Georgia

Caryl & I think of you often. Hope you find my book interesting.

James

Ms. Georgia Chumley
77 Tony St.
Boaz, AL 35957

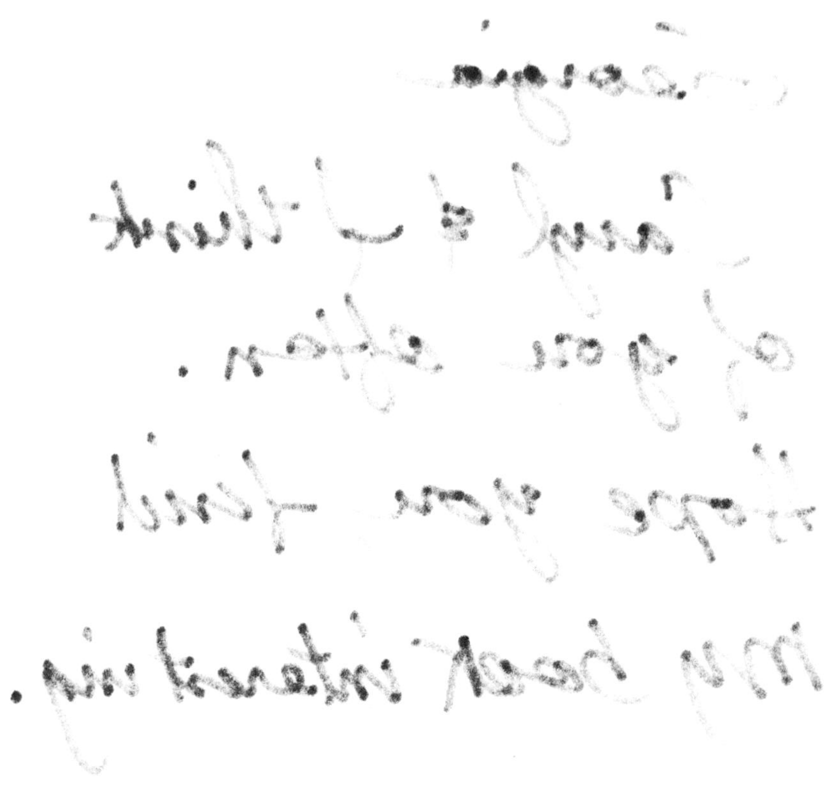

ISBN 978-0-9840463-0-0

Published by Mefford & Ehl, LLC

Justin Hall, cover and layout

Printed 2011 by:
Lighting Sources Inc.
An Ingram Company
www.lightningsource.com
Phone: 615-213-5815 / Fax: 615-213-4725
1246 Heil Quaker Blvd. La Vergne, TN 37086

JOURNEY *to* FREEDOM

Stories of Perseverance and Survival
in the Presence of Great Adversity

Margret Mefford & James Ehl

Table of CONTENTS

FOREWORD

Many Americans have no knowledge or understanding of the extent of suffering and depravation experienced by the German civilian public before, during and immediately after World War II. This book is a compilation of individual stories in separate chapters that recount the experiences of individuals that lived and managed to survive through those difficult and perilous times. This work has been in preparation for two years and the research and stories presented are believed to be factual accounts of individual experiences.

Mostly, this book was inspired by a group of ladies, (now in their mature years), that meet periodically for lunch and to share each other's company. These ladies, from all external appearances, are a group of attractive, charming, highly cultured and exceedingly gracious individuals. The fact that they have all survived incredible adversity is generally unknown and nowhere else documented. Their stories are individual, as none of them knew each other while they were children during WWII or youths when the war ended. Their obvious grace, civility and good manners are astonishing and an inspiration, considering their individual histories. Theirs are all stories of perseverance and survival in the presence of great adversity. Herein are thought provoking lessons for all of us. The material for the chapters in this book was provided by the individuals involved, and initiated primarily for their families, i.e. their children and grandchildren. As such, they contained many personal endearments for their respective families; these endearments have been edited out to more succinctly tell their stories.

The authors considered that with the passage of more time, this turbulent history would be lost if not documented. It is a history that needs to be told and to be preserved for future generations. A message that one can take away from this book is clearly that no one wins in a war or large scale conflict. Even the "victors" lost a generation of the brightest and best of their young men, along with much additional blood and incredible treasure. Even for the soldiers on both sides who survived, many returned home with injuries that would adversely affect them for the remainder of their lives, handicapping their attempts at career and normal living. While this book has a happy ending, or at least a happy present for most of them, there were individuals who were invited to contribute chapters but declined. Their experiences were so horrifying that they simply could not document them for anyone without resurrecting pain that they experienced a very long time ago. This is something that was lamented and regretted, but clearly understood. Some readers may find some chapters of this book disturbing, but all chapters are as truthful and as actual as memory prevails. If anything, time probably has diminished some of the horror that many experienced, but it is important to document their history before additional time has passed.

The following quoted excerpts from a letter, written by German Lt. General Hermann B. Ramcke, while a prisoner of war in Mississippi, details prevailing conditions in Germany immediately following the conflict. It is noted that Lt. General Ramcke was the last commander of the Fortress of Brest, where he was responsible for many Allied prisoners of war. These he treated with great civility and uncommon courtesy, and provided the best medical care that he had available, along with provisions that were equal to what his own troops had. He even moved these POWs out of harm's way when the opportunity became available. The letter was many pages long, but following are the most relevant excerpts:

Camp Clinton, Mississippi
December 25, 1945

There are terrible conditions in Germany - after the hostilities have ceased - such as the death of large numbers of the weak, children and infants, as reported by the daily press, and plundering, rape and mass deportations from districts (i.e. East Prussia, Silesia, the Sudeten) where the Germans have been living for the last thousand years. In addition to the taking over of state property, there has been sanctioned plundering of private property such as a spinning factory, of a peasant s horse, a piece of art inherited throughout generations, or the equipment of a ladies hairdresser s shop (sent home by an American G.I. as a souvenir).

*

There was a distasteful report in the German Press, complete with photographs, on the shooting of General Dostler, who during the con ict ordered the execution of 14 American soldiers who were caught acting as saboteurs (in civilian clothes) behind the lines.

Editors' note: The U.S president ordered this same action for German sailors who landed in the U.S. by submarine. They were dressed as civilians and were on a mission to disrupt the war effort. The shooting of saboteurs and spies appeared to the Germans to be an accepted rule of war and the shooting of Dostler seemed to violate the concept of equal justice, since no Americans were ever punished for the deaths of the German sailors. Every school child remembers the last words of Nathan Hale as the British executed him as a spy during our own revolution "I regret that I only have one life to give to my country". Additionally, George Washington ordered the execution of a British spy, Major Andre during the revolution. Reportedly, this action grieved Washington because he knew and liked Andre, but it was the accepted solution for spies that were caught.

The previous excerpts from Lt. General Ramcke's letter disclose the total devastation of Germany after the war and document the prevailing conditions and the attitudes at the end for both the victors and vanquished. Obviously, it took considerable courage on the part of Ramcke to write this as a POW and forward it to a high ranking U.S. government official. It would seem that Ramcke was a person of noble character who had the misfortune to be born on the wrong side of the conflict.

The authors consider that it is important that this collection of individual histories be documented and published. After all, the history of a nation is the aggregate histories of the individuals that participated (however unwillingly) in the events of their times. As a well known axiom famously declares, "To know nothing of the past is to understand little of the present and to have no concept of the future". We can only pray that history does not repeat itself. The stories related in this book are factual accountings of events that were experienced by the individuals who provided the information for the individual chapters. They relate their experiences before World War II, during the war and after the war. Their stories are ample evidence that even a highly cultured civilization as was present in Germany at the time, can be a very thin veneer. Also, the atrocities (documented elsewhere) that were committed during this turbulent time are ample evidence that some individuals will treat other people very badly if the opportunity arises and if they can believe that there will be no adverse consequences for themselves.

Margret Hoffmann Mefford

James Harold Ehl

Chapter 1
CHRISTEL

"Whatever you can do, or dream you can do, do it!

—Goethe

I always wanted to document the events in my life. I grew up in very modest circumstances, but was blessed with much love and compassion. As the years passed, I have finally arrived at my current status of adult, mother, and grandmother of four. It seemed important to me to record the events in my life, primarily for the benefit of my family. So, over the years, I accumulated a vast collection of scribbled notes (in German) which I stored out of sight in drawers and boxes. This collection became even more voluminous as my memory of events resurfaced. Whenever I could find the time, I would find a solitary place on the beach, the park etc., or even at the work place. My notebook was always with me to scribble a few words, to remember my thoughts later and allow myself to travel into the past, to dredge up from deep within me those long ago almost forgotten memories. I wrote notes in my book, on napkins, even on toilet paper if there was nothing else at hand. I write this for my daughters and my grandchildren, but also especially for me. These are truly Memories from My Heart.

Memories of Happiness and Sadness

The horrible experiences of the Russian Invasion, the tortures and killings, escaping to West Germany from East Germany, crossing the border in 1953, the heartbreaking separation from our families and close friends, living in various refugee camps, not knowing what the future would be, the arrival in the United States in 1955, and the inability to master the English language.

Prologue

I'm sure that my children recall me telling them when they were little girls, countless stories about what it was like when I grew up. They would roll their eyes to heaven because they had heard it a million times. It must have driven them to distraction. Now that my family is older and I'm older, I feel that it is important to write about these events. It has nothing to do with how I grew up, but everything to do with the same feelings we all have in this world, no matter when or where we were born. I believe these are feelings we should share, as much as possible.

As my English language skills improved, I graduated to a manual rented typewriter, an old "Royal". The rental cost was $2.00 per day in addition to the expense of buying large quantities of liquid paper to correct typing errors. But, I still made so many mistakes, so many times that I repeatedly filled the waste basket with crushed paper. I will admit that frustration overcame me again and again and I put everything out of sight for a time. With a busy life, time for concentrating on writing was not always available. But as more notes piled up almost daily, I finally bought an electric typewriter and supplied myself with plenty of self adhesive correction tape. Eventually, things began to get serious with my writing efforts and I typed as much as I could, whenever I could. However, it took me much longer than I expected, not because

I could not remember past events, but because I remembered so much more. My memory kept stretching; moments long ago forgotten became clear almost as if they had just happened. I would wake up in the middle of the night, turn on the light to write some key words in my notebook that I kept on the nightstand. After turning off the light, I would lie there the remainder of the night with my eyes wide open re-living events of the pastc some pleasant, some not so pleasant.

Beginning in January 1999, I made up my mind that I was going to document all the past events I could remember. I wrote approximately 120 pages in longhand, adding words, phrases, erasing, writing again. I began to type all these pages and then my typewriter became inoperable. A friend sold me her's, but that one had more problems than mine, so of course, she returned my money. Both typewriters could not be repaired because parts were no longer available. It became difficult to find an operable typewriter because everyone had gone to computers; it was like going to a pharmacy and asking for leeches.

I had heard of a "word processor" as a possible solution. I saw one demonstrated in a store and was very impressed with all the things that could be done with that machine (WOW!). I soon found out that these things are never as easy as they seem. The thick operating manual was filled with fine print which was difficult for me to read because I needed cataract surgery which I finally had March 11, 1999.

I ask myself, "Why did I want to do this?" I don't know, yes I do! I wanted my family to know my growing pains, dreams, errors, and what-have-you, so that perhaps they can understand (if they should want to) just how I turned out to be who I am. I suppose people never really understand themselves. More than anything, I want my family to understand and know about their grandparents. Hopefully, you will do the same for your own family.

Early Years

My sister and I were both born in Eichenrode/Pomerania. After world war two, this part of Germany became Polish territory. My father's parents always lived there with us, in the same house. I can well remember that house where I was born and lived. My grandparents were the most loving people and I thank God that I had the privilege of knowing them so well and for so many years. Not everyone is that lucky. I overheard my dad talking to my "Opa" that they were planning to move, including our huge dog, a St. Bernard. This dog was such a happy dog. Dad would make some kind of gesture; he would jump up on my dad, place his huge paws around dad's neck and waited for dad to whistle a tune so that they could dance. Dad would tell him "Yodle", come let's dance.

1933 before Hitler came to power was a time of much unemployment and unrest. My father was worried about our future because the national financial situation was very bad. It was common practice to trade among friends and neighbors. My father was blessed with many skills. He would weave baskets and fill them with wild berries we picked in the forest or mushrooms from the meadows and sell them at the market for cash.

In the winter time, our St. Bernard would pull us on our sleds through the village or to school. Later, when we had a couple of horses, my father made a soft harness with shiny ringing bells. A rope would be attached to ours and the neighbor children's sleds and we had a most wonderful sleigh ride. The joyful screams of the children often drowned out the ringing of the bells.

My mother would trade chickens and eggs for dressmaking material and we were among the best dressed girls in our town. My sister and I were always dressed alike even though we were not twins. My mother knitted beautiful sweaters that everyone adored. My grandmother would knit all kinds of items to keep us warm during the harsh winter. The wool would be dyed in various colors so that the knitted items had wonderful patterns.

Christel the Tom Boy

At our county fair, they placed a high pole in the middle of the town square and tied a bunch of hot dogs on the top for the boys to get. Whoever reclaimed the most hot dogs won a prize. As I kept watching them, I decided to try it myself. I had on my prettiest dress but I took off my shoes and socks and up I went. In no time I received my prize of ten hotdogs and a ribbon.

There was a neighbor boy that I was very fond of because he was boisterous. One day he persuaded me to climb through a neighbor's fence and steal some apples. Although we had apples in trees in our own yard, this was more fun because the watchman would chase us but could never catch us because unfortunately he had a physical disability. In retrospect, it was cruel and does not make me proud when I remember this poor man. However, the watchman was not always kind to the children and possibly that is one reason that we engaged in this behavior. Once when we were high up in his tree, we could hear him waving his fist and yelling at us. My friends got away, but my skirt got caught on a branch. As I was trying hard to get away, I ripped my pretty skirt and left a piece of the material behind on the tree branch. I ran home trying not to let anyone see me and changed into another outfit and thought I was safe. My mother was busy in the garden, getting fresh vegetables for dinner and everything seemed to be OK. I saw through the window the watchman talking to my mother and holding a piece of my skirt. I knew that it did not look good for me. My mother was a firm disciplinarian in the best German tradition. She decided my punishment was "hard labor". I was to knead bread and churn butter, for a very long time. It was very tiring standing on a stool and plunging the stick up and down repeatedly.

It seemed that I was always in trouble, even in school. I will admit that whenever it came to playing tricks on the teachers, I was always involved. The results were that I was always the first one the teacher called on. The worst punishment for being a trouble maker or mischievous person was to lie across a bench and have the entire class spank you. It was most embarrassing. No need to document how many times this happened to me!

Baking Bread and Churning Butter

A large brick oven in the middle of the town square served everyone for baking breads and cakes. Everyone received a schedule which we honored unless we needed to trade days with someone. It was very well organized and by baking day, a wonderful aroma embraced the village with heavenly scents. It took quite some time to heat the oven to a glowing red. Coals and ashes were removed into a vat filled with water using a water soaked sponge on a long handle. Using this simple device, the oven was also rid of ashes and dust. The temperature had to be just right and when judged ready, the prepared loaves would be pushed in for baking. Someone had to stand by to watch the whole time the bread was baking. After the bread was baked and the temperature reduced a little, cakes had their turn. When I look back now, it reminds me of pizza baking. I also remember the delights of freshly baked bread with home churned butter.

Every year late in the fall, we had our Schlachtfest, a time when we butchered our own pigs and beef, and made our own sausages, hams, bacon, corned beef and jerky. We would hire help for these activities and chores. Everything was done while singing or humming a song. We children had our chores too, during this busy time. My sister and I loved to make the sausages, hang them on a large stick and place them in the smoke house. The jerky was mainly a snack for school or a treat for our dog.

Barrels were lined up in the cool cellar with homemade sauerkraut, pickles, salted port, etc. I can honestly say with pride, that we lived entirely off the land. There were no pesticides; everything was truly organically grown and picked fresh from the fields or garden, except in the terribly cold winter. Most all of our herbs and spices were grown in the garden, and preserved or dried. Our large attic was filled with trays and more trays of these wonderfully aromatic herbs and spices, some of which we used for tea and others were used for medicine. We never needed an air fresher for the house. We would take our harvested grains to the mill to be ground into flour and also milled into feed for the animals.

We had a few acres of sugar beets. They had to be dug from the ground after the first frost. It was icy cold working in the fields at this time. Some of the beets were taken to a local sugar refinery to make into sugar for us and other beets were used for cooking our very own syrup. It was our favorite on toast for breakfast.

The village had a huge wash house with a monstrous kettle. It was the warmest place in town and a place where all the young people would meet, have fun, sing, and do homework. This was also the place where we made our beet syrup using this large kettle. It was heated for hours to boiling, while stirring constantly to prevent the mixture from burning.

Note from daughter Petra (paper for a school class)

Once I was in Germany cooking dinner. What an ordeal! I had bread baking outside in a specially designed brick oven. I spent hours kneading the bread dough. The grocery wagon had come by our town the day before, so I was able to buy our, sugar, and the other necessary ingredients. I wanted to serve honey later with my homemade bread, so I traded some of my eggs with my neighbor who kept bees. I would also be serving potatoes that we grew ourselves (along with other vegetables), and sausage that we processed ourselves from our own livestock. Since we had no refrigeration, these would need to be wrapped in rhubarb leaves and kept in the cellar where it is the coolest. While I prepared the meal, grandma sat at the spinning wheel working hard to make thread to weave our linens, while the remainder of the family listened to the gramophone and plucked feathers from geese that we would use to make pillows and a feather bed.

Today, I cook the same meal, after I worked all day at the of ce, drove the kids to and from soccer practice and shopped in the grocery store. What and ordeal! Fortunately the meal cooks up quickly thanks to my electric oven, electric rice cooker, and electric bread machine (just push a button and forget it). The sausage was on sale at Safeway so I bought several, some for tonight, and some to put in the freezer for another time. I needed vegetables, eggs and honey, too. It s so convenient to be able to pick up everything I need, all at the same store. While I prepare the meal, grandma works out on the exercise bike while watching television. The other family members are scattered throughout the house; playing Nintendo, listening to CD s, or talking on the telephone.

One of the social changes that occurred between then and now is that the family has moved from the farm to the city. Technology, such as electrical appliances, offers more free time to spend with family or hobbies. People are forced to earn money now to provide for their needs, whereas before, people raised their own food, made their own clothes and linens, and bartered goods for whatever else they needed. Culturally, the progress has driven the family unit further apart as TV, CD players, and video games take them all in separate direction. I m not sure if this is truly progress.

Note: Living off the land in Germany and later technological improvements was not much different from prevailing conditions in the U.S. during the same era.

The Simple Life on the Farm

When I was a child, there were many chores waiting for us after school. Homework had to wait until after dinner. Often we had to do homework by candlelight, or by the light of a lantern. It frequently seemed that the electricity was off. During the summer months, we spent days making jams and jellies. My sister and I had to wash the berries and take the pits out of the cherries. While performing these chores, we ate so much that we often had stomach aches.

We had no indoor plumbing and no running water. Getting water from the pump, carrying the two buckets on a wooden yoke support on our shoulders with two chains for balance, and going the long way into the house was not easy. Water had to be carried in for cooking, washing, bathing, etc. The water would be heated in a large kettle that we also used to boil the linens and for bathing in a large wooden tub. There were no showers except during summer months when we would attach a hose to the pump, hang the hose on a clothes line or tree, while one would pump, the other would jump back and forth to get wet.

When Karl and I went back to visit in 1977, there still stood in the middle of the living room of the old house a six foot tile stove. It would heat the entire house if the doors to the other rooms remained open. It was also used to warm up food. On this stove we would bake apples filled with raisins and cinnamon. A bench was placed next to the stove where the entire family would gather after dinner when work was finished. I always loved that part of the day. We would knit, darn socks, sing, and tell stories. My Oma would usually be sitting at her spinning wheel to make the finest wool thread for knitting. It took her days to prepare the fleece; she had to wash it and comb it into thin layers. She also had a weavers loom for making the finest linens and bedspreads with beautiful patterns. My father also knew how to knit as my Oma had taught him. He created wonderful socks, mittens and even sweaters for us.

In 1938 we moved to Bauer, Germany. That was the same year that our beloved St. Bernhard died. After that, we only had German Shepherds which father trained for us and for the local police. We had one special dog that my father would take to the field or forest in the morning and then send home. Since the dog knew where my father was working, he would take lunch from the house to father in a little basket.

Field Trips with My Father

My father was always training his Shepherd dogs, even when they were little puppies. The dogs were trained for police search and rescue. My sister and I had to pretend being injured or lost by lying down in the meadow or high grass. My father taught me how to whistle using my fingers, which was a skill that made all the local boys jealous. My father could whistle the tune "Edelweiss". That is one reason that I played that song on the violin for my wedding. Every time I hear that song, I think of my dad. Once, dad came upon three small wild piglets in the forest whose mother had been shot dead and was lying nearby. He brought them home and we cared for them; feeding them cow's milk every two hours. Only one piglet survived. We named him Mohrchen, which means black. He was later given away because as an adult he became dangerous. My Opa had 200 sheep and a couple of trained dogs to keep them in boundaries. Many times we would follow him to the pasture and surprise him with freshly baked cake and a thermos of coffee.

My mom had a beautiful voice and was always singing, no matter how busy she was or how hard the work. I grew up in a home filled with music and prayers. My father had prayers for all occasions and for every meal and bedtime. There was very little talking at the table during meals, only my parents would exchange some whispered words. After the meal ended, everyone was talking about the following day, planned appointments, school schedules and necessary transportation arrangements. As we only had one bike and one horse, mostly we used public transportation. If we went to a larger city, we knew the schedule for the last ride home and were always careful not to miss the last train or bus. We knew the routine and what we had to do, and we just did it.

1944 was a bad year for our family. Our home burned to the ground in March. A total of six families were homeless that cold night. My little sister Anita almost died. She was only eleven months old and was almost suffocated when pillows and blankets were piled on her baby buggy as we fled the burning house. Additionally, we received a letter from the army that my father was missing in action, but four weeks later he returned home. We were thankful to God for his return. In the interim, my mother had shed many tears.

I remember my school days, sitting next to Anneliese. She never looked as if she combed her hair and was always dirty. One day my sister and I had itching heads. As we sat in the bedroom, picking bugs out of our hair and dumping them on the floor, our mother entered the room. She was very upset and immediately went to the pharmacy to get some strong solution to kill the lice. It did not only get the lice, but also removed a great deal of our hair and blistered the skin. Mom, in her panic, had not read the label directions to dilute the solution. We suffered from the solution for some time afterwards, but we had no lice!

One day as we came home from school, we heard a cuckoo calling which was a traditional sign of spring. We ran home with excitement to tell our mother that this was the signal to throw away those thick, itchy woolen stockings.

The Russian Invasion

After Hitler began his wars, the first few years went well for Germany. Towards the end of the war, things were decidedly different. I have tried to forget the Russian invasion. It was horrible for all of us, and the unspeakable events that did happen are undeniable. On May 9th, 1945 I celebrated my 13th birthday. This is a day that is still with me as a movie in my mind; an event that I relive over and over. It will never go away. We knew that Russian troops had taken Berlin, but that city was many miles away and hopefully they wouldn't reach us at all. My clear memories are of church bells repeatedly ringing alarms, and the mayor on his horse galloping down the street warning every family. There was great turmoil among the villagers. All of the young men were off at war and these were difficult times for mothers and children. Rumors spread that the Russian troops were torturing and killing people. We tried hiding in the forest, but were spotted and seized. There were beatings, women were raped and some even killed. On May 9th 1945 (my 13th birthday) I was raped by 5 Mongolians soldiers and so was my mother.

We had packed some belongings to hide in the church with other families. There was much prayer, but we soon found out that even in God's house there was no safety. We were found the following day, were beaten and raped repeatedly again, this time by drunken Russian soldiers. They came to our village by tanks, horses and thousands of soldiers on foot. They severely damaged the church building, destroyed all of the grave markers, and posted a sign on the church door, "Closed for Good, Do Not Enter".

It was a dreadful time for my mother, with four children to care for; the youngest still a baby. My father had earlier returned to the war after his leave in 1944, but had requested an assignment in the west. He was captured and placed in a POW camp; as the war ended he was fearful of returning home because of the savagery of the Russian occupation in our zone, and especially the hostility toward former members of the German armed forces. He kept begging my mother to escape to the west which was not as dangerous for civilians. It was easier to escape at that time because the division of Germany into the four zones of occupation was not firmly established and totally enforced. The borders at that time were established but tight control was not rigidly enforced everywhere; however, mother was very afraid to take that risk, especially with four children. We knew that a few families had made it safely across the lines to the west. Mother was in agony knowing that father would put himself in danger by coming home, if she did not flee west. Father did come home after the Russians left our village, but in the year until they left, there was nothing but terror, brutality and fear.

These nightmare memories frequently return, even though they are frightful and painful, and I try to block them out of my heart!

Violence, rape, starvation, nothing but fear and sorrow because so very many women and young girls were raped repeatedly. Many others were tortured and killed. All our livestock were stolen, butchered, and eaten by the Red Army. Chickens, rabbits, and even our pigeons were killed by the Red Army for food. Once, we survivors were all herded together in a big barn. The Russians took not only our livestock and food, but also all the houses, making them their headquarters. Several families had to live together in very small cramped spaces in the barn. Everything that was in our houses was destroyed and many of our belongings were scattered in the street. Feather beds were slashed and thrown out, which caused feathers to fly all over the town; the Russians found this amusing as they drank their vodka. In their drunken condition, they behaved like uncivilized savages; grabbing women and children, laughing, drinking and raping until they were exhausted and fell to the ground. If anyone resisted, they would be tortured or shot. We went into hiding in the attic, but the cries of my two year old sister gave us away many times and the horror for us would start again. Many times we would try to hide in the hay loft and be covered with hay and straw. The Russian soldiers came with their swords, piercing the hay, stabbing women in the legs or other body parts. Their screams and shrieks were constantly with us and are still with me in my memories. For the Russian soldiers, it all seemed to be a game, a sport to be enjoyed. They cared nothing for anyone and they were totally unrestrained by their officers in the pursuit of their savage pleasures. I truly wanted to erase this terrible time in my young life from my mind, but the flash backs still come, even now. I know that they always will.

We all tried to stay strong and to survive this unspeakable ordeal; life had to continue. Being occupied by the Russians, we all had to live now by communist rules; we had to follow their orders, we all became slaves. Schools and churches were closed in the horrible year of 1947. Before the closing of our 800 year old church, my classmates and I were confirmed in that lovely old church. Any kind of religion was strictly forbidden, but the praying went on even harder. There were no more Harvest Festivals (Erntefest), dances, games or fancy pot luck suppers.

People had to find their own entertainment and do their own bible reading. We gathered in homes and garages for praying and dancing. Kurt and Horst played wonderful accordion. Everyone enjoyed it and it lifted our spirits and refreshed our dark somber moods.

We never knew what happened to our beloved teacher Willie Riebe. We all knew that he was a Nazi for we saw his uniform in the closet in the school hallway. We never knew if he was taken away and killed or possibly transported to Siberia, as many were. Most of these we knew that were taken away never came home. I had entered first grade in 1938 where our teacher taught us all about Hitler. He came to power as the Fuhrer because the German nation believed him when he promised jobs for all and food on the tables. For my young generation, Hitler was the "Almighty". Life was good as my parents would say. In 1942 when I was a young girl only ten years old, I was chosen to go to Berlin for Hitler's birthday celebration. Hitler was so inculcated in our young minds that we believed and followed him; we didn't know any better. We were instructed to greet official people with "Heil Hitler". To us it was nothing more than greeting other people with "good day". I remember precisely one day, it was a couple of days after the Russian invasion, I met the beloved teacher on the street, lifted my arm with fingers straight out and greeted him with "Heil Hitler". He bent down to me and in a soft voice asked that I not greet him that way. What? This was the greeting that he had taught us for five years. I was only 13 years old and didn't know better. I'm sure that the first Russian I met, I greeted the same way.

During the occupation, for an eight hour day of work, one could receive a three pound loaf of bread. Our family consisted of seven people, my mother who was very ill, my grandparents old and not well, my sister Luzie twelve was sick with epileptic seizures, and my two young sisters were not old enough to work. I was the only one in the entire family that was able to work. My duty was to shift and shuffle grains in a barge used for storing wheat and rye. I wore my grandpa's big boots so that I could fill them around my feet with grain. We ground this to make pasta or simply boiled it in salted water to eat it as a hot cereal. Earning one three pound loaf of bread daily for seven people was not enough to maintain life for all of us. I always felt lucky to get away with my pilfered grain in the boots. I always carefully watched the guard to be sure that he was at the other end of the building when I filled my boots. One day as I walked like a slow motion robot with my heavy grain filled boots, I had a gun stuck in my back. I stood there frozen unable to move. That day there were two guards, one of which I had overlooked. He pressed his machine gun into my ribs and said "stoy" (stop). He turned me around and in a very soft voice ordered me to dump my stolen grain. He was a good looking young Russian, but even so, my enemy. That same night he knocked on our door, all smelly drunk, gave me a loaf of bread and over his shoulder he had a butchered sheep. He wanted my mother to cook the sheep for him and his comrades. They ate like pigs and drank large quantities of vodka. It got so scary and loud we were all shaking with fear. They must have enjoyed the meal because from that day onward, mom had to cook for this entire wild bunch. Luckily because of this, we were never hungry again and also had ample protection from bodily harm. They usually got drunk, fell all over the place and stayed the entire night. We never knew their intentions, and therefore had many sleepless nights.

The Russian troops left our area in 1946. Activities such as dances and happy celebrations began again. Now our part of Germany was under communist rule and the German people were hired by the government. Everyone struggled to get ahead, learning trades, etc. Slowly, following communist rules and job opportunities we all became separated. There were no phones, and a letter took 5 or 6 days to reach home or a friend. Parents died or moved away and for many friends, all contact was lost.

In 1947, in October, there was an announcement that in Hohensee the very first Erntefest since the war would take place. My friend since the first grade, Kathe, asked me to come along with her. We were both 16 years old. Although this part of Germany was Russian ruled, we were free from harassment and the constant fear that had been present earlier. Everyone was in the middle of the dance floor, but I had eyes on a young man somewhat older than I. His name was Karl and he was working at the bar. I did not see him again until one year later when I was 17. I was in an apprenticeship in Zinnowitz to learn the hotel business. I was allowed two off days per month and on one of these I decided to ride my bike the 40 miles to go home. About half way there, I became tired and got off my bike at a soccer field. I did not know who was playing or even anyone there. From the field came this young man that I had earlier seen at the Erntefest. He just said "Hi, my name is Karl".

We talked briefly and he asked me if he could come to my house that evening to see me. I told him that I would be at the Schloss with friends to see a movie. I did not expect him to come, but was pleasantly surprised when he did show up. Karl had served in the army under Rommel; was captured by the English and was a POW in England. Eventually, Karl had been sent to the U.S. while a POW. In 1947 Karl was returned to Germany to the Russian sector, because his home town was in that sector. Karl came to visit me in Zinnowitz because I could not get any more time off. By Christmas of that year Karl and I became engaged and were married in 1953.

Karl had a job in a uranium mine in Aue. My plans were to move to Aue to be with Karl after the wedding and after I finished my apprenticeship. I was sure that I could find work in a nearby hotel. Karl and I wrote to each other every day, but mysteriously, letters from Karl stopped arriving. Since there was no phone and letters took five or six days there was no way to understand why Karl was not writing to me. I finally did receive a registered letter from the mine. The miners had all been arrested. They had staged a strike for not receiving the essential food necessary to continue with their physically demanding tasks. Everything was on food ration cards. One could only buy whatever was on that coupon. If some of the items were not available, a substitute was made. For butter, one got sugar instead. If meat was not in the stores, one could get an extra loaf of bread. Seldom was there milk or cheeses available. This was how it was all over the communist sectors of Germany. I had earlier given my ration card to my family because I had plenty to eat at the hotel. The miners needed nourishing food because of the physical work and they decided to stage a strike. It was planned to be a peaceful strike, but there is no such thing under communism!

There had been no word about Karl in seven months and finally I wrote a letter to the president of the D.D.R. Herr Walter Ulbricht in Berlin. Finally after two months I received an official letter from Berlin bearing a presidential seal. Karl had been arrested, convicted, and sentenced to five years in a concentration camp. This action was justified under the law that bans "boycotting, militarism, racial hatred, or threat against the government". Also, during his interrogation, it became known that Karl had been in England and the United States as a POW. They also found an address from a friend in England, so a sentence as a spy was added to the other offences. We knew that Karl was incarcerated for all the wrong reasons, but under communism, one doesn't have to have a reason. The state decides. I wrote another letter to the president requesting a visiting permit. My request was granted. I was able to visit Karl in June 1952. I was only allowed to visit Karl every six months.

Visiting with Karl in Prison

It was an eight hour train ride to the Waldheim Federal Prison. Once at the prison, I was guided to a tiny waiting room with four metal chairs, one chair for each visitor allowed that day. A tiny spy hole in the door opened occasionally and a guard kept on checking on us. This was the same guard that would bring Karl to the visiting area. Karl was behind a thick glass wall and the same offensive guard sat directly behind him the entire time allotted for visiting. My name was called and I was signed in and seated before the glass wall. Karl was told only ten minutes before that he had a visitor and he was not told who. The visit lasted only ten minutes before Karl was led away. I was strictly ordered not to tell anyone about this visit. I knew too well not to take the risk. In a communist society, I knew what the consequences could be. Karl was allowed to receive one letter per month not to exceed 20 words. His mother and I alternated our letters. We were also allowed to mail Karl one two pound package per month. We always sent fresh fruit and vegetables. Karl told me later that all his letters were opened, inspected and stamped: Inspected by (Name & Number). Also, by the time Karl received his fruit and vegetable package, it was not editable. It had been cut to pieces, discolored or rotten.

I could see that under the communist system, only those with influence were able to have some semblance of an acceptable lifestyle. My mind worked overtime trying to think of how I might become more political and thus more influential in the system if ever I was to help Karl and therefore myself also. I decided to pretend that I believed in that communist garbage. I joined the union at my hotel and managed to be selected president, probably because of my phony frequent and outspoken support of the system. This allowed me to be present at meetings and conventions. Later, I took over a children's group called "Young Pioneers". We formed a musical group, traveled to different cities, and even performed in Berlin at a "Folk Music Festival" where we came in second place. We all had our picture taken and were congratulated by the East German President, Walter Ulbricht. We also received an award signed by the President.

My thoughts were "If I write him again, could I possibly influence him to release Karl?" Obviously Ulbricht was a German citizen, but we all knew that the Russians were really in charge. I gave it my very best effort, begging him to please lessen Karl's sentence. Knowing the system and the possible consequences of such a petition, I had to be very careful how I worded such a letter. I ended up writing and destroying letter after carefully worded letter until I thought that I had done my best. After mailing my final effort, I could only wait and hope for a miracle. I visited Karl's mother often and at the same time visited my parents. This time was very stressful for all of us, especially Karl's mother.

Finally after a long wait, a letter arrived from the president's office in Berlin. I unfolded the stiff presidential stationary containing the seal of his office. The letter stated "Your request will be honored and processed". That is all that it said.

My summer at the hotel was extremely busy. I had foot surgery and also volunteered to work extra shifts at the hotel filling in for missing employees. One day as I crossed the court yard, to get supplies from the storage room, I saw our maintenance man talking to another man. I heard him say "There she is". Karl had come to the hotel looking for me.

We never knew exactly why he had been released. That summer, there had been riots in Berlin and other East German cities. These had been suppressed by Russian tanks, guns, and water cannon. Many were killed and thousands arrested. My petition to the president might have been the happy answer because of my efforts or simply the jail space had become over crowded because of all the rioting in the streets. In any case, we were grateful that he had been released. Instead of the seven year sentence, he had only served one and one half years, truly an unjust punishment for only wanting enough food to be able to do the heavy manual labor in the mine that the regime demanded.

Karl in Prison

During his investigation, which continued for more that two months, the guards would wake him in the middle of the night, usually around 2 a.m. They would escort him to a very large, almost empty room where the only furnishings were a very long table with one upholstered chair. At the other end of the table was a very short stool. The large upholstered chair was for the interrogator and Karl had to sit very low on the stool at the other end of the table. The interrogator was always at a higher position than Karl, to make the prisoner seem more oppressed and less humane. One wall was painted the color of the communist party (red) and on the other walls were communistic themed paintings, posters, and flags. For hours the interrogator would shine a very powerful and painful bright light into the prisoner's eyes and Karl was forced to look straight ahead. It was painful and blinding. This torture usually went on until early morning. All the while, the prisoner was bombarded with intense questioning. When Karl was finally released, it was with loss of honor, which meant that he would not be able to vote (as if that meant anything!).

After prison, all of Karl's personal belongings were confiscated and he was sent to a work place under constant observation. He was not allowed to look for a job on his own, and he had to report to the police every week. Karl was not free; he was imprisoned in his own homeland. My mother pointed out to me that we had no future in our own country. We earnestly desired to get as far away from East Germany as possible. Karl desperately wanted to leave, but later told me that he was not absolutely sure that I would go with him. I gave him my assurances that I would go with him anywhere and would never leave him.

The Wedding

Our wedding date was set for August 15, 1953. My parents had no idea about our other plans, secret plans of escaping. There was absolutely no way that we could tell anyone. We could have been reported, therefore we lived in fear. Two days before the wedding, my mother tried to talk me out of the wedding, saying that we had no future together because of Karl's past. Only our closest relatives and some very close friends were invited. Our wedding ceremony was performed by a justice of the peace. Afterwards, we partied with much singing, dancing and beer. We spent the night at my parents' house and the next day pretended that we were going away on a honeymoon. I was deeply saddened that we could not tell our parents our secret plans. We were determined to cross the border to West Germany, even though we knew that it would be risky.

Since Karl's job was in Aue and we would normally change trains in Berlin, to avoid suspicion if we had an inspection, we purchased tickets all the way to Aue. In Berlin we got off the train and immediately contacted friends of our parents that lived near the Alexanderplatz, which was not far from the border. We could not phone them because there were no phones and letters were all opened and inspected. We stayed with them for three days, checking the border guards, their shifts, guard dogs, etc. We knew that our friend had full knowledge of the border and had helped others get across. He did it out of brotherly love and concern for his fellow citizens. He put us on a train in East Berlin and told us to get off at the Bonhoff Zoo, because that was the last station before reaching West Germany. Everyone had to get off anyway, for a very thorough and intensive search and inspection from head to toe. We saw guard dogs sniffing at luggage and border guards with machine guns. We had changed into a second set of clothing on the train, left the suitcases behind and managed to get away from the inspection confusion at the checkpoint. We climbed an embankment and were immediately met by uniformed guards with machine guns. We had no choice but to surrender. We were confused and exhausted, and did not realize that these were West German guards reaching out to us with a smile. We had reached West Germany! We were free and Karl and I were together! These guards gave us a hug, welcomed us to West Germany and directed us to a refugee collection camp; "Marienfelde". It was Karl's birthday and we considered it a wonderful birthday present! At the camp, there was help for us everywhere.

Unfortunately, the camp was organized so that men were in one building and women and children in another. We considered it a small sacrifice in order to gain our much needed freedom and we knew that this arrangement would be only temporary. Karl and I met every day in a little park and we met many other couples there too. Karl and I helped out in the camp kitchen and were each paid 50 cents per day. One day as we walked past a delicatessen, we counted our change and we had just enough to buy a small jar of pickled herring. It was uplifting just to be able to buy some food that was not from the camp kitchen. It was a wonderful treat. The living experiences in the camp were not perfect, and I marvel that we were all able to get along so well. In our building there were many nationalities, young people, old people, babies and even sick people, yet we made it work. Since no one had very many clothes, we all had to wash clothes practically every day. There was no hot water and no running water anywhere except in the community wash house. We all washed clothing almost daily and hung them to dry over our iron bed frames. We just did what we had to do. We all had to hope for the future. To relieve the tension, we once had a contest to determine who had the best decorated bed. Even in this stressful situation, it did produce giggles!

The authorities constantly cautioned us about the dangers of talking to strangers. Some individuals were extremely friendly and were promising residents of the camp good jobs with good pay and an apartment. It was extremely enticing because that was what all of us in the camp were hoping to achieve as soon as possible. These people were agents of the East German communist government (DDR) and were trying to lure people back across the border. It happened to some people who believed their promises and they ended up in a DDR jail. Karl and I stayed very alert at all times, essentially not trusting anyone. We were approached by two men who were extremely friendly, but Karl and I did not respond. We later found out that some individuals who were residents of the camp had been kidnapped and forcefully returned to the communist east. We were later approached by two individuals who claimed to be American F.B.I. agents. We did not know what an F.B.I. should look like and their credentials meant nothing to us. The Red Cross assured us that they were indeed who they said they were and wanted information on the torture that Karl endured while incarcerated in the Waldheim prison. They were also looking for information on two American border guards that were also imprisoned in Waldheim. These two guards had crossed into East Germany by mistake and were being held for spying. Karl did know about some Americans or English speaking men that were together in the prison court yard every morning for daily exercise. Karl also met them in the workshop where he had to cut fur for hats. Talking to each other was forbidden, but when the guard walked to the other end of the building, they exchanged a few words in whispers. Karl could speak only a few words in English and the Americans didn't speak many words in German, but they were able to understand each other. The F.B.I. questioned Karl for more than an hour. He told them everything that he knew in order to try to help these unfortunate men.

Our parents had no knowledge of our situation for three months. Our friends in Berlin wrote them that we had tried to escape to the west, but had no other information. They never received the letter. All mail was opened, inspected, censored, and destroyed if the DDR decided to do so. We understood the worry of our families, but since Karl did not report weekly to the police, they contacted his mother and she was told that we had escaped to the west. They gave his mother a bill for 1200 D Marks, a tidy sum. They stated that since Karl was released on parole, he owed that amount to the Waldheim prison. If Karl had spent the entire time in a luxury hotel, the bill would not have been this large. Thankfully, no one in the DDR tried to collect this vast sum from Karl's mother. Eventually, we were able to exchange letters with our families, but all were opened and labeled "inspected".

While still at the Marienfelde refugee camp, we went to the American Consulate to request information about immigrating to the United States. Our papers were checked and also the report from the F.B.I. which the consulate had. We were told that we had a very good chance to immigrate, but it would take some time and we should be patient. They advised us to get medical papers and x-rays taken. Karl had earlier told me about his experiences as a POW in the U.S. and about the lifestyle most Americans seemed to enjoy. We both knew that we had no future in Germany, and I readily agreed to Karl's wish to immigrate to the U.S.

We were moved to another camp and had heard nothing from the American consulate. The new refugee camp was in Aurich near the North Sea. We notified the consulate of our change of address and waited. This camp was in a former army base and was beautifully landscaped. We shared a room with three other couples who seemed older than we. One couple was from Zennowitz and lived on the same street where I had lived. Our assigned living area was a sunny large room with large windows and plenty of space. It contained bunk beds with new firm mattresses. It was a great improvement over the Marienfelde camp.

Exploring the City of Aurich

As we walked along the streets, we saw a help wanted sign in a window. I applied and was hired to help in a kitchen and in a field harvesting broccoli. It was November and very cold. We needed warmer clothing but could afford nothing. There was an organization which is the equivalent to the American Good Will Organization that handed out used shoes and clothing. They kindly provided us with very serviceable, but very worn clothes and shoes. We were determined to earn some money to buy new clothing and some other needed essentials. The pay at our new jobs was minimal, but by working for a restaurant, the meals were heavenly, and much different from the camp food. Also a new wonderful tradition I experienced; tea time. At 3:00 p.m. work was interrupted, the tables were set with china cups, sugar, and cream and everyone's cup was filled with steaming hot tea that smelled so wonderful. It warmed the whole body from the outside cold.

Eventually we received news from the American consulate asking for x-rays because the ones we had earlier submitted were not very clear. We sent new ones which were rejected because mine showed spots from a recent bout with pneumonia. We would have to wait another six months. One day at the camp, I was called to the office and was hopeful that they had word from the consulate, but it was a huge package from the C.A.R.E. organization which was sent through the Red Cross. It was wonderful and they come once a month after the initial delivery. We felt as if we had Christmas every month. We also received help from the Salvation Army which was much appreciated. To this day, these two organizations are my favorite charities.

After a long wait, we again heard from the consulate. We needed to answer questions concerning why we escaped, why was Karl imprisoned, and what was the reason we wished to immigrate to the U.S.? There were also many other additional questions to answer.

Once again, we were transferred to another refugee camp, this time it was Massen in Westfalia. We were asked what part of West Germany we would like to go. We requested the Rhineland and did not specify any city. We requested this because the Rhineland is the industrial heart of West Germany and we believed that we would have a better chance of getting jobs there. We learned that Massen was designated as a release camp and was the final destination before being resettled in West Germany. At Massen, we shared a room with another couple, Gertrude and Helmet Schmidt. The room was so small that one had to climb into bed if another wanted to pass. There was no heat and it was freezing cold. However, we were able to afford a small hot plate to heat water for tea or soup. The bathroom, like all the other camps, was shared by several families, with cleaning schedules posted outside on the door. At this camp, we were unable to get a paying job as we were all waiting to be moved again, hopefully to our final destination. Finally, after several months at Massen we were loaded into a bus and taken to Wuelfrath, a tiny town near Dusseldorf. It was a beautiful area and there were plenty of jobs available.

We were excited and very happy that finally we would be able to get a job and make some money. We finally arrived at our destination, a very ugly building in Wuelfrath. It had boarded up windows and was called the Glass Palace. It was our fourth camp and we believed that things would improve. Even though, the housing was ugly, we were still encouraged. We were young, in good health and we had each other and if we could get jobs, we would be away from this place all day. Not everyone was so fortunate. As we left the bus, we were greeted and handed a number which was the designation of our "stall" as they called it. To me it sounded as if had been decided that we were livestock.

The Glass Palace

When we found our stall, it was just beside a giant furnace which was in the hall. Our stall had no windows and the wall separating all the stalls was just cardboard held in place by thin wooden strips. Occasionally, someone would come home drunk and fall thru the wall into the next stall. Since our stall was beside the furnace, we were warn, sometimes too warm. The height of the upper bunk bed in the stalls was level with the height of the wall, so one could shake hands with the individual in the next stall and wish them good night. In retrospect, it was a funny way to live. This facility housed sixty families and only had two bathrooms, one for men and another for women. We were determined to improve this ugly stall; it was our place. With what little money we had, we went to store sales and bought some cheap material and made curtains and a bedspread. We hung the curtains on the wall and put a flower box beneath with some plastic flowers. Now you could not tell that we did not have a window. Also, we bought some wallpaper to cover the ugly walls. Additionally, we taped some posters to the walls. We thought our place was vastly improved. This was our very first place to be alone as always before we had to share our living space. We were very happy! We had some privacy and could do as we pleased, as long as we were quiet and not disturb anyone. In this facility, the small laundry room was always crowded. There was a posted schedule and bathing was permitted for only ten minutes. Each family had an assignment and a time for cleaning the stairs, floors, kitchen, laundry and bathrooms. Everyone saw to it that the place was clean and sanitary. Everything went as scheduled and no one ever complained.

Kitchen at the Glass Palace

The kitchen was a large space with twin gas burners and was a very busiest place even though there were two shifts assigned. Families with children were assigned the first shift and working individuals used the second shift. In many cases, people with jobs, ate their meals at the factories where they were employed and did not use the kitchen. All the time, we longed for our own place, and our own kitchen and bathroom. We realized that we were all in the same predicament and we needed to not dwell on our misfortune.

Work

Karl and I were called for job interviews and jobs were offered starting the next day. There was essentially no unemployment in our area. To make a good paycheck, the best opportunities were in the factories. It was strenuous work, but we were willing to take anything that would pay well. Both of us worked at the same factory, the same hours and were able to take the same transportation to and from work. Karl worked in the auto parts division and I worked at a sandblast station, treating door handles for all kinds of doors. It was all done on assembly lines. The factory was equipped with a wonderful cafeteria and cost only 50 cents per meal. We hardly ever cooked at home anymore, only on weekends. This saved us time and we were able to get overtime which allowed us to spend more time away from the Glass Palace. The factory also had great facilities with showers, and a laundry room. This was an enormous convenience for us. With our first paychecks, we bought a tiny refrigerator and two speed bikes so that we could get away on the weekends and explore the countryside.

Our lives were improving. Because we both worked, we were able to afford our own apartment, but we had to wait to be approved by the city. The old, sick and families with children had priority on what was available. The entire process was tightly regulated; it did not matter how much money you had. We just had to be patient.

Planning to Move to the U.S.

We never gave up on our plans to move to the U.S. We continued to check with the consulate in Berlin, but we always received the same message that they had no information and that we should wait another two months. In September 1955, we were notified by the city that we could move into our own apartment. It was only a two room place, but it would be our own. We had a combination kitchen, living room and a bedroom. The bathroom was shared by four other friendly families. There was a schedule posted to share the duties of cleaning the floor, stairs and bathroom. But since I worked long hours, I was always too tired for this chore and hired a neighbor to do it for me when my turn came. When winter came, it was very cold so we bought a small electric heater and our apartment was cozy warm. There was a small grocery store in our building and the bus stop was directly out front. We were happy and content. During all this time we did not hear from the consulate and so we began to enjoy the good life, parties, long vacations and buying items that we did not need, but wanted. Unfortunately, we did not feel a need to save money.

In June of 1956, we received a notice from the consulate that we had been accepted to immigrate to the U.S. We were to be in Hamburg and fly to New York on September 29, 1956. We began to reconsider our decision to immigrate and almost daily changed our minds. However, finally we concluded that it was important to begin a new life in the U.S. whatever it was to be. We were concerned about not knowing the language, lifestyle, and culture of this strange land. We sold our furniture, got passports, shots, and gave our parents the sad (for them) news. They had hoped that we would settle permanently in West Germany.

Goodbye to Germany

It was a strange feeling leaving everything and everyone that we had known behind us. From the sale of our belongings, we were able to pay for our airline tickets. We had been told that we could pay when we got jobs in America, but that was not the way we were used to doing things and we did not feel comfortable having a debt. When we filled out the Red Cross papers to request a sponsor, Karl requested auto industry and that is the reason that we ended up in Detroit. On September 26th, we took the train to Hamburg in order to have a few days sightseeing before we left for that far away foreign land. It was my first time on an airplane. The landing in New York was overwhelming; all those magnificent skyscrapers. It was also my first time to see a colored person. He loaded our luggage into a taxi that would take us to Grand Central Station. Everything was new and exciting, but we were well aware of the language barrier. When ordering food in the cafeteria, I tried reading the signs, but I pronounced them as you would in German, which tended to cause confusion. The final solution was to just point.

Grand Central Station was truly an experience. I had never seen a building that was this big. It seemed that we might be on another planet. The taxi driver told us to wait and someone would call for us. Well, a name was called that sounded almost like ours but we decided that it was not us so we ignored the page and kept waiting. Finally someone approached us and kindly asked our name. He took us by the arm and led us to a well dressed man and introduced us to the Rev. Charles Lange.

We truly could not believe how friendly, kind and helpful everyone was. All those years in school, we had been taught that the U.S. only had cowboys, Indians, and criminals. Criminals could easily hide in this land because they never had to report any changes in address to the authorities as we had to do in Germany. With this lack of control, the authorities would be unable to locate them. This was taught to every generation of school children until the German reunification in 1989. Pastor Lange embraced us and with a big smile welcomed us to the U.S. He led us to the train with a colored person carrying our bags. This porter was very friendly and wished us a pleasant trip.

Our ten hour train ride was done in silence as Karl and I were very tired and the Pastor fell asleep. The nine hour time difference was telling for us.

Detroit

We were greeted by Lange's wife Miram with flowers and a hug as she met us at the station. She said in German "Herzlich Willkommen!". One of the German ladies from their church had taught her this greeting. This effort to greet us in German we found very touching. People did so much for us, seemingly just to try to please us. She also asked us if we were hungry. The next day we were greeted by the pastor's assistant, a Mr. Padmus. He also greeted us with a few words in German (he thought) but we could understand none of it. As we shook hands, he had his other hand in Karl's hair making a motion of scissors. He meant that Karl needed a haircut as men's hair in the U.S. was worn much shorter than in Germany. In Germany, a short haircut was worn only by prisoners. Two days later, Padmus arrived with scissors and a clipper and cut Karl's hair much shorter. Karl's only comment was to the effect that if this was the style in this country, then so be it. A few days later, a friend of Lange's gave a dinner in our honor. We were touched about the way they accepted us into their society, their homes and their lives. We both wished that we could converse better and express our feelings and appreciation. We felt that they received our message of heartfelt thanks from our expressions from the heart.

There were other people at the dinner party. Some spoke a little German because of their ancestries. Later, we learned that these people were of German Jewish ancestry. They clearly had no ill will towards us and realized that we were only children when Hitler committed the holocaust against their people. After the prayer and before we began the meal, the host stood, welcomed us and wished us luck for our future. We were overwhelmed with the kindness that was being showered on us. We were brought to tears because of the care and friendliness of the people in our new found land. It was unexpected and nothing we had ever experienced in Europe.

In October the pastor told us to pack our suitcases and he would take us to his summer house in Grindstone, near Lake Huron. Grindstone was a retirement community as well as a summer residence. It was a very pleasant trip in the pastor's huge town car. When we reached the cottage, we were greeted by Harry and Mitzi Guenther. They were former German nationals that the pastor had sponsored two years earlier. Harry had developed a construction business building houses in Grindstone. He had several houses to complete before the harsh northern winter began and Harry and Karl worked from dawn until dusk to finish these houses. Mitzi and I cooked, made plenty of coffee and actually helped, handing them materials and tools. The pay was excellent. One day we went into town to buy new warmer clothes and treated ourselves to our first hamburger and milkshake. All these strange foods were wonderful.

The only heat in the cottage was from a fireplace that also had a grill for barbecuing. Every weekend, Pastor Lange and Mr. Padmus would come up to Grindstone, bringing the largest steaks we had ever seen. He also always brought wine that he claimed was left over from the communion service. After the meals, Lange would change to sloppy clothes and either mow the lawn, go fishing or sometimes help Harry and Karl with the construction work. Grindstone had a large trailer park that was managed by Mr. & Mrs. Whaler. Soon it was Thanksgiving week and we had no idea what Thanksgiving was. Soon we met Annemie who was of German decent and she explained it to us. It was like our Harvestfest. Everyone was invited to the Whalers to celebrate and it was a grand occasion. There was plenty of turkey and tables were laden with strange desserts we had never seen before; pumpkin pie, mincemeat pies, etc.

We left Grindstone before Christmas that year. The pastor told us that he had found us a home with an elderly widow who lived alone. Her home was beautiful. Mrs. Kuhn greeted us with a lovely smile and a big hug. Her house was decorated for Christmas and she already had some gifts under the tree with our names on them. It was our first Christmas in the U.S. We were a little melancholy because we were so far away from home and our families. We were thinking about our loved ones in Germany and we knew that they were thinking of us. There was no way to call them and the mail took weeks. Mrs. Kuhn was of German ancestry and she tried to speak a few words to us in German but once again we did not understand. However, she was very patient in helping us learn English. She was also very anxious for us to have a conversation with her in English. She had grown tired of us just nodding our heads. We watched television with her every evening. Her favorite shows were Lawrence Welk and Ed Sullivan. We shared her house but we had our own bedroom and bathroom. We paid her $10 per month, which was exceedingly modest and all that she asked. She said that this was to help her a little with the utilities.

We also assisted Mrs. Kuhn by running errands for her and driving her to the doctor once a month. She always expressed gratitude. She had an antique 1928 Ford car in her garage that had not been out of the garage since her husband had died 20 years earlier. With a soft cloth, she would walk into the garage, look at the car for a minute or so, wipe the car gently as if giving the car a hug. We saw her do this many times; it seemed to be a ritual for her. We shoveled snow from the front of her house and also from the neighbors' houses. The neighbors all knew who we were and many went to great pains to slowly talk to us. We were frustrated at not being able to fully converse with these kind people. After the Christmas holidays, we registered for English classes three nights each week. We understood much already, but were not so skilled at speaking. Learning English was not easy, but I was working overtime on it, and so was Karl. Our motto was "practice makes perfect".

Employment

The second week in January 1957, Pastor Lange called to tell us he had arranged job interviews for us. Karl was hired at a sandblasting factory. It was hard dirty work but it paid well and that was what we wanted. Karl also took a second job and did not get home until 2 a.m., so he was unable to attend English classes. He only got four hours sleep each night and he did this for two years. The only rest he had was on weekends. Since I had experience in the hotel business, I was hired by the Masonic temple, helping with cooking, serving and cleaning. There were many fancy celebrations, elaborate weddings, birthday parties and other events. I was receiving such good tips that I could buy us groceries for an entire week. If someone else was sick or needed an off day, I volunteered to work. I even scrubbed bathrooms. We both saved as much of our pay as we could. The only time Karl and I saw each other was early morning for breakfast and on weekends.

We saved enough to buy our very own car, a 1954 Ford. I took driving lessons and received my driver's license. We were suitably impressed, because in Germany only the rich and some doctors were able to afford a car. Karl also eventually passed the test for a driver's license. Our lives had changed for the better, better than we had ever imagined.

Our Own Place

In 1958, we decided to look for our own place and found a lovely three room apartment on Hickory Street, a very nice neighborhood. Utilities were paid by the owner and our rent came only to $65 per month for a furnished three room apartment. We told Mrs. Kuhn that we were moving and it was evident that she was very sad. She asked if there was anything that she could help us with, but we declined. She asked Karl to move her sewing machine into her bedroom for her, which he gladly did. She surprised us with some beautifully embroidered linens. She asked us for one more favor before we moved, she wanted us to remove the china from her cabinet and wash it for her. It had been setting there unused for more than twenty years, since her husband died. Karl and I took great care placing them in warm soapy water and when we tried to lift them out, the glue holding the handles from all the tea cups dissolved. We were shocked and very embarrassed. Mrs. Kuhn only said that they were old and she had a feeling that they would break.

We were looking forward to moving and having privacy. Our lovely neighbor across the street invited us to a "potluck". We did not know what this was, but Mrs. Kuhn made a dish for us. We thought that a pot luck must be a big deal because the place was crowded with all the neighbors there. The tables were filled with much food and dessert. Everything was decorated with balloons and she had set up a stage with a microphone. We kept watching the events unfolding and were most curious as to just what was happening. We were finally called to the stage in total bewilderment. These neighbors were giving us a "welcoming to the U.S. party" and were giving us many wrapped gifts for our new household. Also, among the gifts was a bible in German. Needless to say, we were overcome with emotion and thanked them all profusely in our best English while tears ran down our cheeks. Many people from our church also helped us by giving us furniture, clothing and other items. The next Sunday, we attended church with Mrs. Kuhn and Pastor Lange called me down front and had me read a passage from the bible in English to demonstrate how well I had learned English in only one year. He told many funny stories about our stay with him when we didn't really understand English very well and often did inexplicable things trying to understand and please him and his wife.

A New Life

We were able to afford a sewing machine and I advertised for work as a seamstress; I made children's clothes and did alterations of all kinds. I also took in laundry doing uniforms for doctors and nurses. They liked them hand washed, starched and ironed. I usually did approximately forty uniforms each week and I was able to give up my job at the Masonic temple.

One day at the supermarket, we met another German couple, Hans and Ingrid Stuhldreer. Ingrid was pregnant and had to give up her job. Hans was in the construction business, trying to become self employed. Ingrid worked for V.D.O. Service, an instrumentation repair firm. She gave me the name of the superintendent and said that they were looking for someone to replace her. After leaving a message, he called and we scheduled an interview. Karl and I were both immediately hired to begin work two weeks later. We were trained to clean and repair dashboard instruments for cars and trucks of all makes.

All the employees at this firm were former German nationals and we became great friends with all of them. Susi came from Austria and was always bringing in some fabulous desserts. Eva was the best baker I ever knew. Rosemarie was a candy freak and so was Hildegard. Their desks always contained chocolates which they shared freely.

We were in touch with Eddy Ewald, who had been a U.S. soldier stationed in Germany. He was a good auto mechanic but wanted to move to Detroit and asked us if there were openings in our firm. We were able to get him a position with V.D.O. Karl became so skilled at his job that he became the best electrical technician at the firm and often taught others.

Karl and I had the same hours and arrived home usually about six in the evening. I would make dinner and we would do other things. I became pregnant and had to leave the firm in my 8th month. In those days there was no maternity leave. My replacement was Salome who had been born in Austria. I trained her on the requirements of my job and we became good friends. The firm gave me a wonderful baby shower with many fine gifts.

We moved to a larger apartment because we needed more room for the baby when she arrived. We found a lovely two bedroom apartment on the second floor of a very nice house with the landlords living on the first floor. Again they were exceptionally gracious people. Mr. & Mrs. Mathews were always trying to help us, even bringing baked goods to us upstairs. When our daughter Petra arrived, it was my first time in an American hospital and not knowing how it worked, I was lost. Karl was away from work on an errand for the firm and I decided to drive myself to the hospital when labor began. I had earlier spoken with a nurse and she told when the time was right I should come to the fourth floor which was the maternity floor. I parked the car and ran in and walked up the entire four flights of stairs, forgetting to take the elevator. Everything went just fine. Petra was born half an hour later.

When Petra was ten months old, we took a vacation back to Grindstone and rented a cottage from Mrs. Whaler. It was a wonderful relaxed vacation. We visited with Pastor Lange when he was in Grindstone for the weekend. After returning home, I continued doing hospital uniforms and stayed home with Petra.

In 1961, we received a wedding invitation from Salome, the lady that had taken my position at the firm. It was a most elegant affair. There we met Heinz and Rosel Jantsch. We promised Salome that we would return the next morning to help her clean up all the rented glass and silverware. We did and as we washed, Petra kept singing, "Bier her, Bier her, order Ich fall um" (give me some beer or I will collapse) which was a German tune that Karl had taught her. This woke up Heinz and Rozel. After this initial meeting, we became friends and always stayed in touch.

In 1962, Karl received an offer of a position as an electrical technician from a firm in California. Karl had never liked Detroit because of the humid summers and swarms of mosquitoes. Karl took vacation leave from his firm and we drove to San Francisco, California, having an automobile accident on the way but we were uninjured and the car only suffered minor damage. Upon arrival, Karl went to interview for the offered job and with a firm handshake, was hired. The salary offered was higher than Karl was making in Detroit but we soon found out that everything was more expensive in San Francisco. We were delighted to move from the harsh winters of Detroit to the pleasant weather of California. We felt as if we were in paradise.

We found an apartment or flat as it is called in San Francisco, on the upper floor of a very nice house. The lower floor was occupied by the Deutschers. He was a taxi driver and she was a nurse. They both worked different shifts and we hardly ever saw them. Our flat was unfurnished, so we had to have our furniture shipped from Detroit and buy other things that we needed. When Karl started his job, Petra and I returned to Detroit by Greyhound bus in order to pack our belongings for shipment to San Francisco. The bus trip took five days. After everything was packed and shipment arranged, Petra and I took the bus back to California. Shipping the furniture cost $800 which was a significant sum and we had to pay cash. We had no established credit or even a credit card; every expense was paid in cash. It was the German way.

Easter Surprise

As we were leaving Easter Sunday to take Petra to the zoo, we opened our door and there was a huge basket with fruit, chocolates, Easter eggs, and a stuffed bunny with a card attached with the message; Happy Easter from your neighbors downstairs. I was moved to tears. Petra was excited that the Easter Bunny knew that she had moved to California. We were finally aware that the family downstairs was at home and meeting them, hugging them and thanking them was heartwarming. We soon became good friends. Our household belongings finally arrived from Detroit and we felt complete now. While Karl worked, Petra and I would spend time in the parks, beach or at the marina; our favorite place. Petra made many friends and was content.

Petra loved to take walks down our street. One day while walking to the corner to get ice cream, we passed a help wanted sign in a window. We went inside to inquire. It was Happy Heaven Nursery, a pre-school for children aged 2 – 5. The discussion went well and the owner needed someone immediately, so I was hired and went to work the next day. Petra would come and stay with me in the nursery and we would get snacks and one hot meal each day. There was a huge playground with all kinds of equipment and toys. This was really a happy heaven for Petra. The owner had hired me because she wanted to take a three month vacation, but after she returned I only worked an additional week and had to look for another job where I could also take Petra.

Beauty School

I had always wanted to become a hairdresser, even since my childhood. We checked out schools in the area and they were costly. They required

1600 hours and $1200 to complete the course before taking the state exam for a cosmetology license, but it was something I felt that I needed to do. I met wonderful people at the school. Some of these were gay men who were friendly and very artistic in their profession. This was a first time for me, but they were human beings and I just accepted them for who they were. I was the oldest student in the class but I wanted to learn quickly and was a very serious student because of the expense of the course.

We received a letter from the people that we met at Salome's wedding. They also wanted to move to San Francisco. They sold their house and came out. They spent two weeks with us before finding their own apartment. They both found jobs very quickly. We also had to move because the house where we had our apartment had been sold.

I finally finished school and passed the requirements for a state license. I found a job in a small beauty shop in the heart of downtown. Mostly our customers were hotel guests, but we also had plenty of hookers too, not all of which were female. What an interesting job that was! I was paid well and the tips were great. I learned that a beauty shop only one block from where we lived was for sale. The owner was ill and needed to sell and her asking price was reasonable. We reached an agreement and I began working in the shop until I could secure a city business license. I had more business than I could handle, so I hired a part time operator and finally another full time. I finally leased the shop to them because I was pregnant again.

When Petra was eight years old, we took a wonderful trip to Mexico. Later, we also booked a cruise to Hawaii. Everyone got seasick! I just wanted off that ship! We took other trips with our friends over the years; these are all wonderful memories of times with Karl, children and friends.

Out daughter Kristina came along and I suffered from blood clots and required a very long stay in the hospital. I lost function in one arm for a very long time. Additionally, in 1972 we bought our first house. It was a "fixer upper" and needed plenty of tender care. As soon as we were settled in the house, we applied for our citizenship papers. We eventually were scheduled for the naturalization ceremony and our good friends Heinz and Rosel stood with us as they were already citizens. We had tried several times to get a visiting permit to East Germany, but the application always came back stamped "Not Permitted". After trying several more times, we finally received permission.

We flew to West Germany first to stay a few days and wait for our lost luggage. It was our first visit back to Germany since we escaped the East. It was also the first time that our children were able to meet their grandparents. Karl did not go to East Germany with us because technically he had been released on parole and it would have been dangerous for him. Karl stayed in Kiel with relatives. I was longing to see my parents and siblings, but the thought of re-entering East Germany was unsettling. Because we carried Karl's last name; was he still on the wanted list? We had been warned by the American consulate that we would have no protection after entering the communist zone. Crossing the border was harrowing because of the thorough search and extensive questioning.

When we arrived at our destination, there was a taxi waiting for us that had been sent by my parents. I knew the driver well as we had been in the sixth grade together. I greeted him warmly and tried to have a conversation with him but he would only answer yes or no. It finally occurred to me that his was a strict government job and we had been labeled the enemy. He was not allowed to be friendly with us. I quickly got the message. I also knew as a girl an individual named Irmgard who followed us everywhere we went. We had to be very careful because of the stalking and reporting on the part of those who carefully watched us. One wrong move on our part and we would be in big trouble without any protection from the American Embassy. Coming out of a department store dressing room one day, I purposely bumped into her, greeted her warmly by name and apologized profusely. She quietly confessed that she had been assigned to follow us and report to the police. Truly the people's state was an oppressive police state!

My children were shocked at the lifestyle of my parents. They had only known an American middle class lifestyle. My parents had no indoor plumbing or running water. Water had to be carried in and heated for bathing, washing dishes or doing laundry. Even if a family had money, there was little to buy in the stores. There was no TV, no refrigeration, no microwave, and no electric stove. Food was cooked on a stove that used either wood or coal. Clearly, the communist system caused most of the people to live in poverty. It was sad for all of us when it was time to leave, but I am glad that my children grew up in a much better world. We were glad to arrive back home in the U.S. and for us, clearly the U.S. was home. Petra kept saying "I like my country better than Germany".

Leaving East Germany was a nightmare. My youngest daughter Kristina had been affected with a severe allergy. I appealed to the authorities to grant us an additional three days for her to recover, but my request was denied. Her face was badly swollen, red with numerous blisters and she had a fever. The best I could do was to apply a Calamine type lotion and give her a mild sedative to relieve as much pain as possible. When the train stopped at the border for the guards to clear everyone, the guards insisted on scraping off the lotion because she did not exactly match her passport picture. She screamed with pain while the thuggish guards completed their task. I was greatly alarmed for Kristina, but I also knew that the guards had firm orders and would be in personal jeopardy if someone used this ploy to extricate a child from the east. I appealed for medical assistance which was finally granted but not before Kristina was severely traumatized and crying with pain. I knew that many people crossing the border had been shot or at least detained for little or no reason. I was paralyzed with fear. Much later, I noted with some satisfaction (schadenfreude) that when the country was reunited, many of these guards were prosecuted by the unified German government, mostly those that had killed people trying to flee the East.

1977 Trip Back to Germany

Later, we were aware of the Switzerland summit meeting where many changes for the better were made in East Germany. All East German political prisoners were released and their prison terms were erased. They were free to travel. We collected as much information as we could find on the new conditions. Karl was anxious to see his mother and brothers once again after 24 years, if he safely could. We finally decided that we would go. Petra would stay home and mind Kristina while Karl and I went alone.

The trip started with a series of ill omens. On the way to the airport the car hood came loose, flew up and blocked forward vision. We stopped and Karl tied down the hood with a piece of rope that we had in the trunk. The plane left the gate on time but sat on the runway for more than an hour without air conditioning and with the bathrooms locked. We felt jinxed. We finally arrived in Hamburg and spent a couple of days in Kiel with my cousin Ilona.

We took the train east; I knew what to expect at the border crossing but Karl did not. This time there was a remarkable change in the behavior of the East German border guards. There were fewer guards, fewer dogs and not too many machine guns. The guards politely asked us for our passports and even used the word "Please". They returned my passport, but retained Karl's. One guard gave it to another and he walked out of the cabin with it. Karl's face turned ashen. Another jinx? The train started moving slowly and a guard quickly returned and handed Karl his passport and apologized. He even wished us a pleasant journey. Based upon my earlier experiences crossing the border between east and west, this was truly astonishing. However, Karl had been traumatized. The taking of his passport by the guard brought back very unpleasant memories of his incarceration and torture by the East German Government and instantly brought fears of again being imprisoned. Karl was so stressed, that he felt ill. I had three small bottles of schnapps in my purse and we each drank one and gave one to the lady who was sharing our compartment.

Karl is usually the calmest of people, but the passport incident had completely unnerved him to the point of illness. The train gathered speed and we both realized that we were safe. Karl's brother met us at the train station in Stralsund. They had not seen each other in 24 years. Karl had a very good reunion with his family and former friends. Thus began a round of parties, some more intense than others. The parties lasted for hours with some, including Karl, becoming quite intoxicated. This was totally out of character for Karl, but he was so happy to see everyone and they were happy to finally see him again that perhaps some excess was to be expected. I knew that Karl realized that this was the last time that he would ever see his family. The last day before we were to catch our plane to the U.S., Karl came home intoxicated from all the final partying with his family and friends.

We had to walk to a bus stop to take us to the train station. It was raining and muddy. In Karl's unsteady state, he slipped and began to fall. I tried to prevent his fall but ended up falling into the mud with him. As we walked on to the bus stop, Karl was muddy and drunk and I was muddy and very angry. When the bus arrived, the driver would allow me to board but not Karl. I reached into my purse and discretely gave the driver $10. In those days $10 U.S. was an enormous sum in the communist east and much more than a day's wages. The driver deftly accepted the bribe and allowed muddy drunken Karl to board but made him sit up front by the door so that he could quickly exist if he became ill.

The bus ride to the train station was surreal. I was still very angry with Karl for his current state and for the fact that he had caused me to also become muddy. We knew most of the passengers on the bus from our past lives in East Germany, but no one spoke to us or acknowledged our presence. My anger soon dissipated as I realized the true situation. We were former East German citizens; Karl had been imprisoned for protest against the regime, had been tortured as a political prisoner, I had formerly been a minor communist official, and we had escaped at the first opportunity. Yet, here we were in our former homeland with American passports, money and seeming immunity from the local authorities. I realized that there was surely an informer on the bus and any friendly overture to us could possibly cause someone to encounter the same fate that Karl had earlier endured or at least some difficulties with local party officials. It would have been dangerous for anyone on the bus to be friendly to us, even if they were former close friends. I just wanted to return to the U.S. where I knew I belonged. Petra had said it best years ago when she declared "I like my country better than Germany".

We went to the station to catch the train to Hamburg. The train ride was exceptionally smooth and the border crossing was without incident. The East German guards even greeted us with a smile. We caught our plane and were overjoyed when the pilot announced that we were over "our country" the United States. We were glad to once again see our children, even though Petra had called us once or twice while we were in East Germany.

Karl kept talking all the way home about his family and how he was so happy to see them again. It was the last time that we both saw our parents. We never again returned to Germany. My parents died in 1983 and Karl's mother died in 1985. Karl's father had died in 1947 shortly after Karl came home from the POW camp. Karl's older brother died in 1983 of mysterious circumstances, purportedly from a heart attack. However, we always believed that he was murdered by a communist agent because he was an outspoken critic of the communist government. He had received several warnings about his public criticisms but did not heed these directives. There was nothing anyone could do; no one dared to question the official finding. Karl's other brothers allegedly also died of a heart attack. Karl's brother Heinz had just gotten off a bus when someone suddenly injected him with a needle (poison?) and he fell to the ground. The official finding was heart attack. Karl's sister Hildegard also died very young under mysterious circumstances. Clearly East Germany was not a place to live unless you could accept the communist philosophy or pretend to do so as I had earlier done. I never felt good about my earlier deceptions, but I had adopted this pretense to help Karl get out of his dreadful imprisonment where he was tortured daily.

Christel's Beauty Nook

I missed my beauty shop which I had earlier sold after my first return trip to German when my children were small. I missed being a hairdresser. I saw an advertisement for a small shop for sale that was very close to our first address in San Francisco. It was large enough for only one and one half operators. It was an area I knew well and had parking just outside the door. I made arrangements to meet the owner and Petra and I went to see it. I paid $500 for the business, but the place was a total filthy mess. Petra and I went to the store and bought a huge quantity of Lysol to fumigate the place and kill everything that was alive and crawling. The furniture and equipment were trash. I was afraid to touch anything or to sit on any of the furniture. We removed everything including the floor covering and replaced everything top to bottom. We thought that it was a vast improvement and it certainly was clean and sterile. Many of my clients from my first shop returned and most of the previous clientele also stayed. It was a great place for business which I had believed when I bought the dump.

My old customers from my first shop were glad to see me again and in a very short time my appointment book was filled. I hired a part time operator for weekends and holidays. Petra came to the shop after school and helped me do small tasks. She was of enormous assistance, answering the phone, making appointments and doing other small things that were allowed without a cosmetology license.

Not all my clients were loveable people. As is well known, San Francisco is the home of some very colorful characters. One regular who came in every week was a "Sophie Tucker" impersonator who occasionally performed in small theater and clubs. At the time, Sophie had been dead for many years and we always wondered how she could be successful if the person she was impersonating was essentially dead and unknown. She always came to the shop wearing a huge black cape, which made us think of a bat. She had a habit of requesting to use the phone which was located at the cash register and she always shielded our sight with her ridiculous cape. Every time she used the phone, there was cash missing from the register, the last time it was $45. We confronted her, which caused a most unpleasant scene. We recovered the cash, showed her the front door and told her to never return.

Another woman had been our client for many years; however I will admit that we did not like her very much. She never seemed satisfied and always had some minor issue to complain about. One day she had what could only be described as a complete melt down. Half way through the process, she started screaming that she was disgusted with the Nazi. She emphatically stated in a very loud voice that no daughter of the Nazi was cutting her hair. Further, we were all Hitler's helpers and should be made to wear the swastika on our sleeve as the Germans had forced the Jews to wear the Star of David. I do not know if she was reliving the horror of the holocaust or if perhaps something else had set her off. In any case, I was furious with the scene she made and showed her the front door and instructed her to never return. It was unfortunate because she had been a regular who lived in the neighborhood. Even though she tended to be difficult, we took no pleasure in baring her from the shop. Who can say what horrors she had experienced during the war, but the scene she created upset both me and the customers who were present and was very bad for business.

After several years, I sold the shop mainly for health reasons and because we wanted to move farther south to San Mateo to hopefully find a climate that was a bit warmer. I found a position as a nanny and did some cooking for a delightful family with two children whom I came to greatly love.

Epilogue

In retrospect, sometimes I wonder if perhaps God, for our transgressions inflicts partial punishment on some of us while we are still alive. We have all seen individuals who have experienced great tragedies. While the Bible does not say so explicitly, a very careful and thoughtful reading of the scriptures could possibly allow this conclusion. Conversely then, one could also conclude that perhaps God might direct some good things to some individuals. My theology is questionable in these thoughts, but it is comforting to me. I have always believed that there is a God who created the universe and all mankind.

With these thoughts in mind, could it be that I was given Karl as a gift from God for the loss of my childhood by the thuggish, uncivilized and brutish Russians? When we first started dating, I told Karl about being seized and my subsequent unspeakable maltreatment by the Russian soldiers when I was only 13 years old. Unexpectedly, Karl did not treat me as a "fallen woman" but rather expressed great sympathy and caring concern. This brief conversation assured Karl a place in my heart forever. Karl never mentioned this to me again, even though I have never been able to forget it. So, I have asked myself repeatedly; "Is Karl a gift to me from God for the loss of my childhood, inflicted on me by the incredibly cruel Russians?" In any case, I was smitten. In my heart I knew that Karl was meant for me.

Later, when Karl was sent to prison by the evil East German Government for political disobedience, I was personally devastated, more so than ever before. That is the only reason I decided that I would pretend to embrace their uncivilized and illogical system to try to make it work for us. I would do whatever I could to gain political influence so that I could possibly help Karl. Within the dysfunctional communist system, one had to have influence to get anything done. We all knew that Karl was enduring torture at the hands of this cruel regime. I quickly worked my way up to union president at the hotel where I worked. No rational person would want this position, because it meant constantly responding to the inane directives of the local communist government officials, who can best be described as buffoons. It did enable me to join the politically active Young Pioneers, a truly useless organization, because Germany had no lands to pioneer. However, through this connection, I was able to take my "pioneers" to Berlin to a folk festival where I managed to meet the East German president and be photographed with him. Then I began my letter writing campaign to the president to determine if I could help free Karl.

This campaign was fraught with peril. It was dangerous to criticize the government or to charge the government with making a mistake. I could only state that Karl was a dedicated supporter of the proletariat government of the people, and only by his influence was I inspired to join politically active organizations to better our glorious homeland. I also diplomatically stated that while Karl was at work the day the miners decided to strike, it would have been personally dangerous for him alone to have opposed a group of hardened miners and thus he was taken with all the dissenters when the authorities took action. I kept repeating these themes in several letters to the president, while diplomatically speaking of the time I had met him in Berlin.

We never knew if my efforts helped, or perhaps Karl was freed after 18 months for other reasons. There were riots in several East German cities and the jails were full. We do know that his treatment in prison did not become better until just before he was released, which was about the time that I received the final permission letter from the president stating cryptically that my request would be granted. While in prison, Karl had no knowledge of my efforts in his behalf and was not informed until he returned home.

Out of prison, one day Karl tentatively and very hesitantly suggested that perhaps we might be married someday. He was met with a resounding YES, any time he wished. Karl told me later, that he realized that he had no future in East Germany because of his status as a convicted felon, even though it was a political crime. He was very unsure if I would marry him. He need not have concerned himself; whatever menial job he had to take and however poor we were destined to be, I just wanted to be with him. Besides, in the communist system, most people were poor. Only party officials lived well and they were all carefully selected toadies of the Russians. I had grown up in very modest circumstances and I knew how to cope.

My family repeatedly tried to dissuade me from marrying Karl, but I was not listening. After we made plans for marriage and before the ceremony, once more Karl tentatively confided to me that he wanted to escape to the West. Once again, he told me later, he didn't believe that I would marry him and try to escape. If we were successful, we faced the bleak possibilities of never seeing our families again and the difficulty of trying to assimilate in an alien culture. If we were caught trying to escape, then we both were destined for long prison terms. Karl need not have worried. He was again met with a resounding yes and I began to help him plan for the escape try. We believed that just after the marriage ceremony would be the most opportune time. We did not even tell our families. The entire escape experience and later living in refugee camps was extremely stressful, but we are here now, where we wanted to be. With the changing times, we are free to visit our families in the reunited Germany whenever we wish and can afford to do so.

Petra married and in good time presented us with two delightful grandchildren. Eventually Kristina also married and we had two more grandchildren. Our daughters and their families were greatly loved by Karl and by me; however, after 18 years it was clear that Petra was unhappy and her marriage was crumbling. They were divorced in March 1998.

Karl, truly the love of my life, died suddenly April 24, 2005. He passed away from an abdominal aneurysm within 20 minutes of being stricken. We had been married 52 years. We had endured many trials and hardships but we had worked very hard and were always happy with each other. I now spend my time enjoying retirement and my grandchildren. I readily acknowledge that life for us was not always easy, but because I could be with Karl, most other things seemed unimportant. I know in my heart that Karl was truly a gift to me from God, and so were you, dear children.

Chapter 2
MARGRET

History of Kassel

When did all this begin? The world was still relatively peaceful when I was born in September of 1938, to Erich and Gertrud Luise Alexandrine Hoffmann. We lived in the city of Kassel, Germany, where most of mother's family had lived for hundreds of years. Kassel is located in north-central Germany and is well known for its one-of a-kind beautiful mountain park, Wilhelmshöhe. A powerful local aristocratic ruler, Landgraf Karl, visited Italy in the early 1700s and was so impressed by the Roman waterfalls at Tivoli and Terni fountains that he wanted to build similar structures on the wooded hills near Chasalla, as Kassel was called in the year 913. The structure that dominates the hillside high above the park and castle is a gigantic octagon with the statue of Hercules on top, which is the symbol of Kassel. Over a distance of 250 meters a waterfall cascades over steps downward into a large pond. At night the whole structure is illuminated and can be seen at a great distance. The Emperor Wilhelm II designated the Wilhelmshöhe castle as his permanent summer residence.

Today the castle serves as an art museum with seventeen Rembrandts among its hundreds of other masters on display and is recognized as one of Germany's foremost museums. The brothers Jacob and Wilhelm Grimm of fairy tale fame also lived in Kassel from 1838-1841. They traveled around the countryside collecting stories that had been told from generation to generation but never written down. Besides fairytales, the brothers also engaged in studies of German linguistics, literature, law, history and mythology. Hand-written manuscripts can still be seen in the Brüder Grimm Museum in Kassel. One of the most valuable possessions of the museum is a personal copy of the "Children's and Household Tales " with handwritten notes by the brothers Grimm.

The first wallpaper museum was established here in 1923. All the public buildings of earlier times were of distinctive architectural baroque styles not used in modern structures and, therefore, in my opinion, exceedingly beautiful. Sadly many of those buildings were destroyed during the war and not rebuilt in their former style.

Family History

My father came to Kassel from Essen, a large city in the northwestern part of Germany where the Krupp Industries were involved in iron, steel, coal and heavy defense manufacturing. My grandfather, Peter Hoffmann, worked for Krupp all of his life. He and grandmother Katarina died in 1948. I remember them vaguely since I was very young when we visited, before the bombing of German cities became an everyday occurrence. Grandfather Peter held me and showed me a yellow stuffed canary over their bedroom door and told me that I could not touch him because then he would fly away. I watched for grandfather to come home from work and then I got to sit on his lap and was allowed to pick out anything I wanted from the food on his plate. They lived in a very affordable rent housing area built especially for Krupp workers. There were two small bedrooms, a living-dining area combination, a kitchen, a bathroom and a small balcony.

In Kassel the days were filled with mother and grandmother

Petronella, visiting Eduard and Luise König', my great grandparents on my mother's side, going to the park, feeding swans and ducks and enjoying the beautiful flowers. This particular park was called Karlsaue and adjoins the Orangery, which served as a summer residence for the Landgraf and his family. In winter some of the adjoining buildings were used to store plants that cannot withstand frost and later these buildings became an indoor botanical garden. Since this park was within easy walking distance of the great-grandparents' apartment, we spent much time there. (Perhaps that accounts for my love of beautiful gardens and flowers.)

My grandmother's maiden name was van der Brock and the family came from Holland in the early 1800s to settle just inside Germany in the small town of Füssenich. When she married Wilhelm König, an accountant, they moved to Kassel where Mother and her brother Helmut were born. My grandparents were divorced in 1930, I believe, but shared the raising of their two children with Eduard and Luise König, my great-grandparents on my mother's side.

When Mother and Father married, they moved into an apartment that was furnished with Mother's dowry money and things she received from her family. Then the war came, my father was drafted and only came home on leave once in a while. When the bombing started, the apartment was destroyed and mother and I moved to the great-grandparents' home. The furniture in the apartment and everything else was gone except a few pictures and the jewelry Mother owned.

Marriage

How time flies! Wasn't it only some weeks ago that I had to complete papers in English and German and make four copies of each? Then I had to give them to the American military offices in Germany to be processed, since Bobby was a member of the army of occupation. The wait to hear whether they would approve our planned marriage was several months. When the provisional permission finally arrived, there were appointments to be made to visit the chaplain for an interview and to schedule a medical checkup; only after all positive reports were received would the American military grant final permission to marry. One really had to want to be married to that particular soldier and be willing to wait before wedding arrangements could be made.

I kept asking myself, "Was this really what I wanted?" It all seemed so bureaucratic, so businesslike and so contrary to the romantic notions I had pictured in my teenage mind. In those days most girls my age were looking forward to getting married someday, having children and living in a nice home without the thought of having a particular career. To be a wife and mother had always been my dream. Of course we had our dreams of how handsome the soldier would have to be before we would choose to marry him and much of our time was spent just talking about that dream soldier. When my best friend Edith and I rode around on our bikes and the GIs whistled at us and called us "baby", we were surprised but always flattered. They noticed us, we thought, and kept on riding, smiling and hoping that they would talk to us. They usually did. We were pleased that we could use the English language skills we had learned in school and so we listened very attentively to what they said to us. We found out very soon that not all of them were our idea of a boyfriend and we decided then that we would only talk to those GIs who were our idea of handsome and also nice.

So, the next time someone asked us something and he was not what we considered "just right"; we just acted as if we did not understand English and rode away quickly. So the months passed and we went to the German movies with some of them and to a snack bar to eat pizza, something we had never had. Once when it arrived at the table I mistook the olives for grapes and thought to myself "How crazy is this, grapes on a pie that is not a pie"? I associated the word pie with a sweet dessert, just as we had learned in school. Soon it became clear to us that there were many things the GIs told us we never learned in school.

Edith had an older sister who was engaged to an American in the Air Force and her father worked at the Rothwesten Air Base for the Americans. All this activity concerning their engagement and the forthcoming wedding took place over a few months time in the summer and then I had to leave return to Essen where my family lived. I only visited my grandmother in Kassel during summer vacation. Now that I have been involved in planning several family weddings, it is clear to me that we were spared an enormous amount of stress and expense that we would not have been able to afford.

When the paper for final permission to marry arrived at my home it was Wednesday, as I recall. I called at Bobby's work, something that usually was not done, and the man who answered called Bobby to the phone. I told him that the permission papers had come and asked him what day would be good for him to get a pass. It was agreed that Wednesday the following week was good and I went to make the arrangements. When I saw him on that weekend I told him to be at the Rathaus (courthouse) at 10 a.m. Wednesday and we parted, to see each other again at 10 a.m. on the designated wedding day.

On Monday, my grandmother and I went to town and bought a pretty beige dress with matching jacket that was to be my wedding dress. I still had good shoes and a really nice necklace with matching earrings, which completed my wedding ensemble. On Wednesday I went to get my hair done early at my friend Hannelore's parent's beauty shop. There were no flowers.

For Bobby and me a church wedding was not an option, since no one in our family went to church. Also, we did not have the money to buy an appropriate wedding dress, which is the secret dream of every girl about to be married to the most handsome soldier in the world. So we did the one thing everyone else had to do in Germany at that time; we went to the courthouse in Kassel and were married by a justice, with only grandmother, mother, Ralf and Joachim my brothers, and one of Bobby's friends in attendance. The ceremony was spoken in German and English and that was that!

Bobby came to the courthouse wearing his khaki uniform and I thought that he looked very handsome. His friend, Leonard Daugherty, also came along for "support" for Bobby! As I try to remember what the official who married us said, I find that it bears no resemblance to what preachers say in wedding ceremonies here in the U.S. At times I have wished that we could renew our vows here and I would then have a "real" wedding. But then again, our marriage has lasted over 50 years now and a new ceremony would change nothing. The weather was nice on that 16th of July 1957 and we all went to a nearby restaurant for dinner. Then a little later we went home where my grandmother had made a strawberry pie. It was the first time Joachim (age seven) and Ralf (age five) had a whole bottle of Coca Cola all for themselves; such were the times and economic conditions in Germany. Later that afternoon, Bobby and I went to the Service Club at his Kaserne (barracks) and there we celebrated with his friends and anyone who happened to be present. Since it was a fairly small post they practically all knew each other and we had a great time. Never before in my life had I felt as happy as I did that evening, especially after someone in the crowd said, "How about that, Mrs. Mefford?"To hear my new name made me feel like a queen since now I had a handsome husband, a new name and my little world was complete. Thinking back I wonder why no one, including me, thought of having a camera at the courthouse. It was the expense I suppose, that prevented us from even thinking about it. Then a week later one of Bobby's friends got married at the same place and they had a group picture made with us at the end. So when I got the picture I cut off the other people and it became our official wedding picture at the Rathaus in Kassel.

Our one furnished room we had rented the week before was ready for us and also contained a few things of our own. The $15 a month rent was not too expensive and we did not even mind sharing a bathroom with others. Shared bathrooms and even kitchens were not unheard of at that time throughout Europe, so we did not feel disadvantaged. We even had a two-burner hot plate and there I cooked the things I had eaten at home. They were very simple meals such as Schnitzel, fried potatoes and a salad. I had never made nor served iced tea, since that was not the custom in Germany.

For breakfast, I remember, I once cooked slices of bacon and then on top of that bacon I put the eggs. When Bobby saw that he asked, "What is that?" I told him this was bacon and eggs the usual way I cooked it. He ate everything I cooked for him and only later I found out that some things were not to his liking but he never complained (new husbands rarely do). Once he asked me if I knew how to cook pinto beans and when I answered, "No, what are pinto beans?"; he knew there was no way he would get them while in Germany. Later back in the U.S. his mother taught me how to cook the beans and we have enjoyed them ever since. This was how we lived in Germany and there we stayed until a few months after Susie was born in 1958. We went to stay with my mother and grandmother for about a week before leaving to come to the United States.

Mother and my brothers Joachim and Ralf lived with Grandmother Petronella König in a house in a suburb of Kassel. Mother was 39, strikingly beautiful and had been a widow for about 3 years. After Bobby, Susie and I left for America, mother met and married Joachim Schaumann, an engineer who designed and built bridges. Unfortunately, he died in 1968 and my mother was widowed the second time. Because she spoke perfect High German, was also fluent in English, French, and Spanish and had a working knowledge of Italian and Portuguese, she went to work as an interpreter for a German defense contractor (Wegmann), translating the instructions for the weapon systems of the Tiger tank. Translation was required because this company was exporting these weapons to other European countries.

It was during this time that my Grandmother Petronella began to develop cancer, the cause of her death in 1960. My grandmother had always been a very important person in my life and I had always been close to her. It was a great sorrow for me not to see her again when I returned to Germany in 1962.

My grandfather, Wilhelm König, was a member of the Nazi Party before and during the war. He was the only one in the family who had faith in the government. He was an accountant and had a very good income before the war. It was always to my regret that I never was able to really get to know him since he lived far away in the countryside. I have no recollection of ever having a good time talking with him or of him being affectionate with me and I believe it was because he was so far away and never a part of my life. After the war, he once was asked to leave the hospital where he was treated for some illness because he talked about how Hitler was so misunderstood and was really a good leader. Such talk was politically incorrect after the war. As much as I disagreed with his politics, he should have been permitted freedom of speech. He died at the age of 84.

In those days, wives of American personnel living a certain distance from the American hospital in Frankfurt were required to come to Frankfurt two weeks before the due date. We had to live in a hotel designated for that purpose until it was time for the baby to make its appearance. So I packed my little suitcase at the appropriate time, caught a special military bus and went to Frankfurt. Bobby could not accompany me and I was really hoping he would be able to join me a few days later but, alas, that was not to be. After spending about ten days there in the company of other women in the same condition I was in, Bobby arrived one morning. We had a nice day together, the only one with him present, because that evening Susie began her journey into the outside world. After a quick ride to the hospital on icy streets (it was February and very cold), Susie came the next morning at 5:23 a.m. Bobby came to see us and then had to go back to Kassel to go to work. As I recall, there were 53 babies born in the 97th General Hospital during that night and into the morning. I rested all day and the next day Susie was brought into the room with me and I had to care for her from that time on. The nurses instructed us as to how we were to do things and all the supplies were readily available, but to take care of my own new baby was a challenge! I knew some things about caring for new babies from the time my little brothers arrived and I looked after them with my mother's instructions.

But here a lot of things were really different. The way diapers were put on babies, with pins no less, something unheard of in the German way of diapering babies. In Germany by tradition, one took a square diaper and folded it into a triangle and put it under the area to be diapered with the long ends at the side and the shorter one between baby's legs. Wrapping them over the area to be covered. Then take another somewhat heavier diaper and wrap it around the bottom. Finally, take what we would call a receiving blanket and swaddle the baby in it.

We were required to get up and walk around the next day, take a shower and do things for ourselves. In German hospitals, things were still different and I had much to tell my friends when I came home. After three days at the hospital, I was discharged. The nurses told me that someone would get in touch with my husband and he would be able to pick us up. I had not seen Bobby since the morning Susie was born. How we enjoyed our beautiful baby girl! She had lots of black hair and as far as we could tell, she had brown eyes, which she still has today. We had a beautiful wicker baby bassinet with flowered material draped all around and lying there she looked like a doll. I was so proud to have a handsome soldier husband and a beautiful baby. Grandmother had bought us a German baby buggy. We took Susie for walks and shopping and she was admired by all who looked at her. It was a happy time for us.

Then came the day of our departure for America. When we were ready to walk out of the door for the last time, I suddenly realized again how far I was traveling. When would I return to see these people whom I loved? As it turned out my beloved grandmother would die while I was in America; I would never see her again and my children would never get to know her. Surely those thoughts were mirrored by all who were staying behind. It would be 25 years later when I was the one who stayed behind and my first granddaughter would leave town and my heart ached as never before. Then I recalled the scene in Germany so long ago when I left and realized how much pain my family must have felt.

We left Frankfurt Rhein Main Air Base on a military flight to New York and arrived about 17 hours later. What a shock I experienced after getting off the plane! In Germany the temperature was a mild, almost cool summer day, that sixth of June 1958. In New York the temperature was at least 85 degrees Fahrenheit and the humidity probably 75%, something I had never experienced in Germany in the month of June. Of course, I was dressed appropriately for an important journey such as this: a light gray suit, white blouse, stockings and a hat. As soon as possible I took several things off and was left with only my skirt and blouse and a few necessary items. Susie also had to shed several layers and I was hard pressed to dress her right because I did not expect such a drastic change in temperature. After a bus ride to a military office somewhere in New York City, we rode again on a bus to Grand Central Station to catch our train south. On that ride I saw things that were very new to me, such as homeless people sleeping on the sidewalks. I believed they were homeless because of what the people in the bus said. Even during the worst of the war with all the destruction caused by the constant bombing, the local authorities found somewhere for people who had lost their apartments to live. Living in a German city, I had never seen high buildings with boxes in the windows (air conditioners) and so very much traffic.

We finally arrived at Grand Central Station and went to the waiting area. There were only hard seats and I changed Susie and we looked for water so I could prepare her bottle with the powder formula I used. The real problem was the diapers. I only had cloth diapers and carried the dirty ones in a bag until we could get to Alabama to wash them. What a mess! Finally we boarded the train and were on our way. Little did I realize what a long ride it would be. After many hours in the regular seating area Bobby was able to get a sleeping compartment and we could actually lie down and get some sleep.

The view from the train was very bleak for a long time and very seldom did I see anything really beautiful. I began to wonder what this big adventure of mine would turn out to be. My baby was my first concern at that time and I was too busy taking care of her to worry anymore about what came next. We arrived in Chattanooga, Tennessee, and were met at the station by Bobby's mother, his aunt Esther and his cousin Doris. I had only seen one picture of my mother-in-law and was pleasantly surprised at her appearance and that of the others.

The biggest surprise for me was Doris. She was 19 years old (the same age as I), had a car, a job and was not married. Bobby and I did not own a car. Then another delightful surprise was to see the two older ladies dressed so very nicely. While in Germany I only saw young Americans and so to see these ladies in brightly colored dresses looking so lovely was not what I expected. They were so very friendly and seemed genuinely happy to meet me. I was happy that I understood almost everything they said.

We got into their car and drove two hours to Huntsville, Alabama, where my mother-in-law Ruby lived. There we met a plethora of the other relatives who had come to see us. They had not seen Leroy which is what Bobby was called by his relatives, in over two years and of course that foreign wife and baby had to be viewed. I believe they were surprised that a German, the first they had ever seen or really given any thought about, could speak perfect British English and could actually understand what was being said. All of Bobby's friends and relatives were exceedingly friendly and most kind. Everyone remarked about how much hair Susie had, some stating more than any child they had ever seen, which of course could only have been a southern hyperbole but a very kind one.

Bobby had accrued leave and so we settled in for the duration. Ruby had a wringer washing machine that was a welcome sight for me; I could finally wash Susie's diapers. Actually it was the first washer I ever used and Ruby was happy when I volunteered to do all the laundry. It was a real treat for me to use that washer and then to hang all the laundry out into a backyard with a large clothesline and best of all, warm weather, which made everything dry in record time. No more putting diapers on the line and before the last one was hung out; the first one was frozen stiff.

Another different experience was all the new things to eat. First in the morning there were biscuits and gravy, a very unusual combination to eat for breakfast, at least for me. I had been accustomed to bread or rolls and assorted cheeses and butter and jelly for the first meal of the day but this southern breakfast was very tasty. Then in the course of the next days, there was corn, cornbread, pinto beans and iced tea, very delicious things I had never tasted. Over time Ruby taught me how to cook all these traditional southern dishes. The desserts were also very different. Pies especially were new to me and so very good and the layer cakes were different from any I had ever eaten. I had to get used to eating the white bread and I believe that was the most difficult food for me. There just was no German bread available in Huntsville at the time.

We were invited to different relatives' homes and I met all of Bobby's family living in Huntsville. It was a treat to see all the different houses they lived in, so unlike Germany. Something I especially liked was how friendly all the people were; they all invariably invited us back as we were leaving. The saying "see you later" was a bit confusing at first and I asked Bobby if they meant for us to come back later or did they mean to visit us where we lived. He told me that is was just a polite southern term that most people said when someone left their house after a friendly visit.

One day Bobby's brother, Charles, asked me if I wanted him to "carry" me to the store. The word carry had a different meaning for me and I realized that it was used frequently in the South instead of "take". So over time I was introduced to many new southern aphorisms that had a different meaning from words I had learned in school. The one thing I really missed was public transportation. Everyone had to drive wherever one wanted to go. I could not drive and so was very limited in my moving about. We had a buggy for Susie and I walked her up and down the street where we lived. There was a drive-in restaurant just around the corner and I saw young people, not much younger than I, driving cars, parking there, playing popular music, getting food and laughing; they all seemed so happy and carefree. It was a sight I had never seen before and I noticed the girls all wore pretty dresses and especially black and white shoes. I had always wanted to wear black and white shoes with white socks. Well, I eventually got the shoes and the white socks but it did not do for me whatever it was I thought it would.

My young happy ever after dream shattered when I found out in July that I could not go with my husband to Fort Bragg, when he had to report back from his leave. Susie and I had to stay in Huntsville with my mother-in-law. It was not what I had imagined our life would be and I was heartbroken and felt so utterly abandoned. How could this be? But the reality was that we did not have enough money to move away and live somewhere else. That was, without doubt, a miserable time spent away from my husband and living with my mother-in-law, even though she was most gracious and very pleasant. She did her best to console me and cheer me up. We went to the park when someone could come and drive us but it was far from the life I wanted. So Bobby left and Susie and I stayed in Huntsville until early the following year when we were able to move to Fort Bragg, NC. We found an apartment and lived there for a few months but Bobby objected to the cooking smells that other families created and we started looking for another apartment. We found what is called a "shotgun" house in Spring Lake, so called because when you open the front door you can shoot a shotgun through without hitting anything except the back door. It had a living room, bedroom, kitchen and bathroom. We settled in and soon I found I was pregnant and the baby would arrive in November. Nancy was born on the 28th of November 1959. She was so tiny compared to Susie, who was almost two years old. Her hair was very dark and she also had brown eyes. I was thrilled I was to have another healthy, beautiful baby in my arms.

While we were still in the hospital I woke up one morning and I was completely stiff and when I turned my head I experienced excruciating pain. Finally I could move and get up; after awhile I was fine again. What a scare that was, thinking I would be paralyzed! A week before Nancy's arrival, Bobby came home with his arm in a cast and I wondered how he could take care of Susie when I went to the hospital. But it worked out and I was back at home on the 30th of November. The weather was still nice at the beginning of December that year and

I was able to go for walks with Nancy in the buggy and Susie walking beside me. She wore a harness to keep her close, since she was very much a runner. At about the same time, we had a surprise I had not anticipated in my wildest dreams. Bobby came home with orders to go to Korea for 13 months.

Again, I had to move to Huntsville to Grandma Ruby's when Nancy was two months old. We actually got a three bedroom apartment in a newly built complex and moved in with some of my mother-in-law's furniture, since all we owned was a car, a baby buggy and some dishes and our clothing. I really did like Ruby but my life was not at all how I wanted it to be. I had a husband but who gone in a country with only his relatives and no friends of my own. I suppose I did feel sorry for myself for a while but not long.

I became angry at being there and not knowing how to drive so I could get out and see other things with my children. I got into our car that was parked in a back parking space, found out how it worked and then went to get a learner's permit. I practiced driving every day until after two weeks I was ready to get my license. I passed the test and had a license. Then our travels began; we went to the Big Spring Park and fed the ducks, which was Susie's favorite activity. She would have gone to visit them every day if I would have taken her. We were able to go to the commissary, doctors' appointments and so many other places and I was no longer depressed. Of course, I missed Bobby and counted the days until he would return. I had a large picture of him and I always told the girls that it was their daddy, hoping they would not forget him. But when he did come home after thirteen months, only Susie remembered him. When Bobby tried to hold Nancy, she started making an unpleasant face and did not want him to hold her. It was several days later when Bobby and Susie started to get their coats to go out; Nancy motioned for me to get her coat also. From that time on she was fine and began to be friendly with him. He had returned in March of 1961 and, after some days of leave, we went back to Fort Bragg with him. How happy I was when it was just the four of us and we could be a family together again.

But our happy life was to be short in duration and the day came in July when he came home with orders for Germany but not with family. So back to Huntsville we went and stayed with Ruby for a short time until I could get my own apartment with the girls. There was always the possibility of us going once the Berlin situation was settled, then dependents could begin to go to Germany again. The communist leaders in East Berlin realized that if something was not done, there would not be many people remaining in the eastern part of Germany because they were crossing into the west by the thousands every day. They decided to build a wall between the Russian sector of Berlin and the western parts of the city and along the many miles that separated the American and British sectors from the Russian occupied part of Germany. The widespread unrest caused the American government to temporarily halt the travel of dependents to Germany. After three years, Bobby finally received orders to go Germany but we could not go. I spent my time going to the University of Alabama in Huntsville attending citizenship classes. There I met another German lady named Ingrid Jones and we became good friends. It was a great experience to learn in depth all the workings of this country's government. I enjoyed it so much that if I could, I would go through it again.

When we graduated, my friend Ingrid's mother-in-law gave us a graduation reception, which was attended by many of their friends. We had red, white and blue corsages with little American flags and the cakes were decorated in the same colors. It was a wonderful experience; one I will always remember with great delight. I had an American passport and could travel to Germany and back without the hassle of getting a visa ever again. Susie, Nancy and I all had the same passport. It may not mean so much to those who were born here but to me it was a high point in my life; to be a citizen of the one country in the world I had admired for so long and where I wanted to live all of my life. Not long after that I received my orders for travel to Germany, and we set out to fly from Huntsville to McGuire Air Base in New Jersey for a MATS flight to Germany. It was August and very hot here in the States. Just as a last minute thought, I took a light sweater for myself, which was a lifesaver. When we arrived in Rhein Main, it was early in the morning and very cold. The girls were dressed warmly and I had my sweater.

The War Years

The peaceful times in Kassel came to an end one night in June of 1940 when the British Air Force bombed our city for the first time. I suppose it was to be expected after the German Luftwaffe bombed London and caused much damage to the city with many civilian casualties. It was especially disturbing to have the bombers come at night. People had to scramble out of bed to get to a shelter or to the basement. These bombing raids became more frequent during the next years because of the high-value targets in the city of Kassel. Henschel Industries, which produced rail cars, trucks and airplane motors, was located in Kassel. The Fieseler Airplane Manufacturing and also military storage depots were in Kassel. Later, the American bombers always came during the day because their mission was to destroy the factories, which produced anything necessary to fight the war. Regrettably, they were not as accurate as they tried to be, which resulted in and many civilian deaths and the destruction of many homes. The British Royal Air Force always came to bomb at night because their goal was to disrupt the civilian population so the workers could not function very well the next day; therefore, not work as efficiently.

Father was in the German Luftwaffe at this time and Uncle Helmut was a Luftwaffe fighter pilot. At first, Father was stationed in Kassel but when the German military occupied France he was transferred there. He returned in 1944 and was attached to the headquarters in Kassel again. By that time, the air raids had increased significantly, not only were we bombed at night but also in the daytime.
Of course, Kassel was not the only city being bombed; it was every city with any facility to manufacture goods for the war effort. As soon as the bomber squadrons were detected approaching German airspace, alarms were sounded in all the cities they were expected to fly over. We had to be ready practically at all times to run to the shelter at a moment's notice. Even though the planes did not always drop their

bombs on our city, we still had to seek shelter because we did not know just what city would be bombed. So on the occasions when the "all clear" sounded, everyone was relieved. And then came the long way home and in all kinds of weather; we trudged on slower than when we made our way to the shelter earlier.

My father was home on leave one day when the alarm sounded and we grabbed our bags (I was assigned a small bag with my clothes and a few necessities) and ran to a nearby shelter. While there we heard the noise of the bombs hitting the buildings nearby and when it was finally over and the all clear sounded; we walked out of the shelter into a burning city. Smoke was everywhere and we were wondering if the house with our apartment was still there. In Germany, most people live in large apartment houses where one can rent or purchase an apartment. How relieved we were when we saw the building still intact and we rushed into the kitchen to get something to eat. My father went to the open window just looking out when he noticed some loose bricks in the backyard close to the house. Immediately he got excited and in a loud voice (almost screaming as I recall) said, "To the living room, now!" So we all ran as fast as we could toward the front of the apartment and had just reached the living room when the back of the whole house exploded with a horrendous noise. I remember falling flat on the carpet and the crystal chandelier came crashing down right next to me. Mother screamed as she flew across the room and as I looked up I saw father covered with blood from the glass flying all around. We were alive and no one was seriously injured but only the living room was standing; everything else in back of the house was gone. As father said later, when he looked out of the kitchen window and saw the loose bricks he immediately suspected a time bomb, which it turned out to be.

There were other families in the building who had returned from the shelter and gone to their kitchen for something to eat not knowing of the danger and they were dug out of the rubble later. Several of my playmates were also among the victims. It was a great loss as far as possessions were concerned, but we were alive. As a young child my concern was that now all my toys were gone; no more dolls, doll beds, or doll stroller. All the books that I loved had disappeared in one great explosion. Thinking about that today as an adult I see where my parents were the victims, in a greater sense than I understood at the time. It was then that we moved to Frankfurter Strasse to live with the great grandparents. Their apartment was very large and luxurious, with real oriental carpets everywhere and I was assigned the task to comb the fringes of those carpets. No doubt they just wanted me to be busy and have something to do. I also remember a very large painting in the dining room that was a picture of very beautiful flowers and fruit. The ceilings were ten feet high, decorated with plaster decorations and had plaster medallions around the top of the chandeliers. Great-grandmother Luise had a cook and also two sisters who came to do the laundry. Additionally, there was a lady who cleaned and was there to see that all was done for the family. Grandmother Petronella had her own apartment, which was staffed equally well.

Life was still very good in those days. We spent our time at the apartment and visited the park nearby where I fed swans and ducks and picked flowers. Since I did not have any siblings, I was always attracted to other children and mother told me that when I saw the kindergarten children walking in the park, I insisted on being allowed to walk with them for a while. One day when mother and grandmother and I were feeding the ducks, there were some little fish swimming close to the edge of the water where I was standing. I dropped a little ruby ring I wore, a present from my grandmother, into the water and said that the fish were only going to play with it for a little while and then bring it back. That was the end of that little ring. Then one morning as I walked out onto the sidewalk ahead of mother, I saw something that made my little heart really happy; the swans had come to visit me close to my house and brought the lake with them. In the night, many miles away the Edertal Dam had been bombed and destroyed. The result was many houses, whole villages, train-tracks and many animals were destroyed. Over 1300 people were killed that night as the water from the dam rushed in and flooded the area for many, many miles down river. Many hundreds more were injured and scores left homeless. As a child, I did not realize the seriousness of the swans coming to visit. It would be many years before the park would be restored to its former beauty and usefulness.

The air raid sirens became something we had to get used to because they sounded often. No matter what activity one would be involved in, the warning of impending squadrons of heavy bombers appearing and dropping their bomb loads on us was enough for everyone to stop what they were doing, grab their bags and run to the shelter. There was no point in getting into one's pajamas at bedtime. When the sirens sounded at night, it was better to be ready and dressed to run to the shelter; so I went to bed dressed and ready to go. Now there were many tall apartment houses that had basements designated for shelters and, when the bombers appeared sooner than expected, many people went to their basements instead of running farther to the safer shelter of the Weinberg.

The Weinberg was a limestone rock formation in which there were long tunnels, which led to rooms where people could be safe from the bombs that were dropped. Many years before, in 1825, beer brewers dug long tunnels because they found that it was the ideal storage place for beer in barrels; the temperature stayed an even 10 degrees Celsius and the humidity was conducive for beer storage. In 1942 these tunnels were expanded to make a safe place for people when there was an air raid. There was space for about 10,000 people and there were iron entrance doors to this shelter.

Father was seldom able to visit but he had left a radio with my mother so she would be able to hear when bomber squadrons were on their way toward Kassel. And he said for her to go to the Weinberg shelter as soon as the sirens sounded. It was about half a mile away but by far the safest place to be during a bomb attack. The worst time to run to the shelter was always at night because we did not get to sleep. Many times as we were running toward the shelter, the bombs would already start falling starting fires in different places. Smoke and dust were in the air as buildings were blasted apart and, at times, it became difficult to breathe. At night was the time when the bombers dropped what we called Christmas Trees because they looked exactly like that when they were falling. The purpose of those incendiary devices was to show the places where the bombers, that were following, should drop their bombs. Of course no one could predict where the bombs would hit and so running very fast was of the utmost importance. But little legs get tired and at times I just could not run anymore and Mother carried me the rest of the way.

After we finally arrived and found a place to put ourselves down, we were always so tired. The noise of the bombs hitting outside would not let many people go to sleep. My most vivid recollection of shelter life was being wrapped in a fur coat my mother had and lying on the floor, feeling the vibration of the bombs hitting the ground.

One of the most devastating attacks came in October of 1943. It was late in the evening when the sirens sounded once again. While Getting ready to go, we realized the bombs were already falling in another part of town not far away. Also, many Christmas tree incendiary devices were dropped to show the next wave of bombers where to drop the larger bombs. Since the Christmas Trees set things on fire where they were dropped, it seemed as if the whole city was ablaze.

Grandmother Petronella decided, as she had so many times before, to stay in the basement of the house. So we ran as fast as we could to the shelter. We could smell the burning smoke, which drifted in our direction as we went in and the iron doors shut behind us but the smoke smell stayed with us. It seemed as if the bombing went on for hours but later we found out it was just over one hour. More than 400 planes had dropped over 1800 tons of bombs on the oldest part of the city with the purpose of creating a firestorm. That purpose was achieved and the beautiful part of the city was destroyed in one night. The more than 10,000 people who perished did so in most heinous ways; by suffocating in shelters or being burned to death. If one could have reached the Fulda River and stayed there until the heat died down; one might have survived but that was accomplished by very few people.

While all that was happening, we were in the shelter hoping we could get out soon and return home, that is, if our house was still standing. Mother always carried some bread with her and a sharp knife to cut slices off. So on that occasion, she proceeded to slice a piece of bread and accidentally sliced her finger to the bone. I can still see the blood running onto the stone floor forming a puddle. She wrapped her hand as well as possible and then we waited for the doors to open. Finally, we were able to leave but what a sight awaited us! The air was filled with smoke, buildings were on fire, some had just the roofs burning, others were half destroyed and there were holes in the street where we ran before entering the shelter. In the distance, the sky was as red as the most brilliant sunset and we were amazed at the sight. It was the old historic part of Kassel burning out of control and a thousand-year history was burned with it. In the future, to be seen only in pictures and on postcards. Generations of families died horrible deaths that night. There were few survivors who could or would tell of the unspeakable tragedies that took place in the inferno.

Mother was unable to readily locate a doctor to take care of her finger (a small inconvenience in light of everything else). After two days, she was able to find a doctor who did the best he could for her but the finger was never the same again. Mother told me many years later about the never-ending questions I asked and some of them she could not answer to my satisfaction. My questions were: "Why do the airplanes drop bombs on us? Why can we not just put our nightgowns on and go to bed? Why do we have to run to the shelter at night? Where is my daddy? Why were lots of people lying on the sidewalk? Would they get up later and go home? Did the children find their parents and did the parents find their children?" I once saw women walking on top of heaps of rubble that had once been a house and calling their children's names; I asked mother where those children might have gone. Of course, the questions were answered to the satisfaction of a six year old but I remember thinking that those children could be under all that rubble.

It was late in 1944 when the air raids seemed to get more intense and more frequent. The sound of those droning airplanes unnerved everyone every time they flew over and I asked my mother how much longer this would go on but, of course, she could not tell me. We had to bundle up as the weather turned cold and there was not always fuel to heat the apartment. It was a rather large apartment, which consisted of a large living room, dining room, and a large verandah room where the windows could all be pushed to the side to create a summer retreat. There was also a kitchen with a balcony and a large pantry with shelves all around. The two bathrooms were equipped with large tubs where I loved taking baths. The hallways were wide and long, as I recall, because I took my dolls for a walk around the corners of the hall and then walked through the living room to another hall. The apartment contained four bedrooms. There were not any other children to play with, other than the ones we met at the park. There was a library in the apartment with another room adjoining it, which we called Opichen's retreat, where great-grandfather liked to escape the noises of the household. There I would visit him and he would read stories to me and point out pictures in books. As I think back on the times I spent with him, I am filled with such peace and happy feelings and I see him in my mind's eyes. He was a small man with wispy gray hair, glasses that looked as if they were going to fall off any minute and a very soft voice talking to me and telling me stories or answering questions. Mother told me later that he was the one who helped her with her Latin studies and explained things in such a gentle and precise manner that she was able to learn it very quickly. Great-grandmother was the one who gave me a large comb and showed me how to comb the fringes on the many carpets around the apartment.

Another memory from that time in my life was that my Uncle Helmut, mother's brother, came to visit and brought chocolate for me. He was a Luftwaffe fighter pilot and came to see us whenever possible. He made sure to wear a dishtowel around his neck whenever he gave me chocolate, so as not to spoil his uniform. Father also came to visit and both he and my uncle wore the same uniform. Mother told me that once I commented about the fact that I had two daddies who always brought me chocolate. One day I became very sick and after I was taken to a doctor; the diagnosis was that I had scarlet fever, a highly contagious disease. That meant I could no longer go to the public shelter and had to be admitted to a quarantined part of the hospital, which was located several miles away at the outskirts of the city. There were many other children in a large room and my world seemed to end when Mother and Grandmother had to walk away and leave me there. The air raids kept coming but I do not remember any of us in that hospital going to a shelter. We were just there listening to the bombers flying overhead and the loud noise the bombs made when they hit something and exploded. Later I understood the agony of Mother and Grandmother much better; they had to leave me not knowing if we would ever see each other again. The air raids continued and Mother went to the shelter and Grandmother went to the basement. By this time the great-grandparents had already moved to the country where there were no bombs dropped and they remained there until they died in the late 1940s. Whenever possible, mother came to see if the hospital was still there and when I saw her coming I was so very happy to see her. I do not remember how long I had to stay there and never thought to later ask mother.

Winter was fast approaching and my thoughts turned to Christmas. Even though it was war, Christmas could not be prevented from making its appearance. Since there was not a great selection of toys to be found and I loved dressing dolls, mother made me several doll dresses out of father's ties. Also, my father managed to find a little toy store with real packages of food for dolls and a small scale with little paper bags for the groceries the dolls would purchase. For a six year old, it was a dream come true. In Germany at Christmas time, the tree is not decorated by the parents until Christmas Eve. Then when all is ready they ring a bell, the children come in and are told that the Christ Child just flew out the open window but left all these presents for them! How much fun it was to play with my new toys and enjoy not having to run to the shelter for several days. But just as we were getting used to enjoying peace and quiet, the sirens started again. By this time Father was gone and Grandmother and Mother and I were alone in the apartment. It was a very cold winter that year of 1944/45.

On a very cold day, several days after Christmas, the sirens started again and we grabbed our bags and started running to the shelter. Mother begged my grandmother to go with us but she said no; she had stayed in the basement many times before and it would not last long and besides she was tired, it being in the middle of the day when she liked taking a nap. So, grandmother went to the basement along with most of the other residents of the house.

This particular bomber attack was made by the United States Army Air Force. Mother had a fur coat she wore when we ran to the shelter but when I got tired and wanted to sleep she wrapped me in that fur coat and I slept on the ground just as soundly as in my own bed. The lining of that fur coat is vivid in my memory as I write this and I will never forget it. Finally, the all clear sounded and the iron doors were opened and we were allowed to go out. What a sight! It seemed as if the whole street before us was a bomb crater! The air was filled with smoke. As we looked around, many houses were on fire with the flames coming out of the empty windows, others had roofs burning and firemen trying to put out the flames as long as water was available. We started down the street toward our house hoping that it was still standing. But as we came closer, we saw that our greatest fear had come true! Our house was ablaze! It was a very substantial structure but a bomb must have hit it early on and now fire was coming out of all the windows; there was nothing we could do but stand there and watch.

Oh, the agony my mother must have felt knowing her mother was in the basement of that burning house and no way to get to her. People were frantically trying to dig to get to the people who were buried under all that rubble but to no avail. They had to give it up because the whole building was soon going to collapse. There we stood with only the clothes we wore and our bags in hand with no place to go. All my beautiful toys were gone, my dolls, my buggy, and the little store I played with for a few days; all went up in flames along with all my clothes and shoes and everything else we owned. How great a loss it was for my mother and grandmother and great-grandparents, I only comprehended much later.

At that time, the German government required people to list how many rooms they had in their apartments and when someone needed a place to stay temporarily they would have to let them live there. It was a most unsatisfactory situation for the people who owned the apartment and not pleasant for the new occupants of the room. So there we were in a room by ourselves, grandmother's condition was unknown, father was somewhere else and did not know of our situation but life had to continue. After a few days, the rescue workers were able to dig their way into the basement of the house and were able to get grandmother and two other people out alive; at least 15 others were dead. Grandmother was sent to one of the hospitals and started a long recovery period.

In the interim, we continued living in that one room which had a coal-burning stove in it and as long as we could find coal somewhere we had heat, a place to cook something and could keep warm. Father caught up with us at some point and was able to get some necessary items for us before he had to leave again. Food was very scarce during those days and mother had the idea to start digging for the food that was stored in the basement of the house that burned. In Germany, each apartment owner also has a basement space where items are stored. Wooden racks are there to hold potatoes, onions, carrots, cabbages, jars with preserves and all sorts of things to eat. It was a dangerous undertaking since the rubble was very unstable. Mother told me to watch outside and if I did not hear her calling me, I should go for help.

Sometimes she was able to find something to eat and other times nothing. Because of the freezing cold, some of those things she brought out were frozen but we still ate them for lack of anything better. Maybe that was the time I ate cabbage and potatoes a lot and I still love it today. I remember a glass dish on top of the stove filled with cabbage and potatoes or carrots and potatoes and then sometimes there were onions with potatoes. Even in severe adversity, we ate a very healthy diet. Bread was there also and so we did not starve. There were also public kitchens set up all over town with meals for people who had no food and we went there for some meals. Also, clothes were given to those who had lost everything in the houses that had been bombed and burned to the ground.

Later, after the war, I saw pictures in The Saturday Evening Post where children wore white socks. What a beautiful sight! I thought and wished for white socks right away but it would be many years before that ever happened. Another common item we had to try to find was water. Since many of the water supply lines were destroyed, there was no running water where we lived. There were pumps in places and when mother found one not too far away, a half mile or so, she got a sled and a very large kettle and off we went to get water. When we arrived, lots of people were already lined up and so we waited for our turn to arrive. After what seemed a very long time, we got our kettle filled with water and I sat on the sled; mother had me hold the kettle as tight as I could and off we went. Every once in a while we hit a bump and a little water sloshed over the rim on my mittens. After several sloshes my mittens froze stiff and icicles were forming on the sides of the kettle, but we had water and were glad to be alive to go and get it.

While we lived in that room, the air raids still continued and our trips to the shelter seemed to get more and more frequent. In between, we got water and mother still went to the basement to get food. In those days, one lived one day at a time and did the same thing over and over. When the alarm sirens sounded we ran to the shelter, then home, then find food, then get water and, of course, we did not have a refrigerator. The winter being very, very cold that year helped immensely by keeping food somewhat cold but since there was not much food the burden of trying to keep it fresh was removed from us and everyone else also. Then the day came when, after another stay in the shelter, we came out and when we came closer we saw the building with our little room on fire and almost ready to collapse.

So, once again, we stood on the street with only our bags and the clothes on our backs. The only thing to do now was to find another place to stay but that was easier said than done. There were public shelters set up for people just like us who had no place to go right then. So we wound up in one of those shelters, until other arrangements could be made. That was when I developed a terrible earache and we walked and walked for hours, it seemed, until we came to a clinic and I could get medical attention. It was a middle ear infection and whatever they did hurt worse than before. I remember fainting and when I woke, it seemed as if my head was going to come off, it hurt so much. Then we had to walk back through paths where the rubble was cleared from the streets and some of the places were still smoldering from the fires. People were digging in the ruins and sometimes we came to a pile of what used to be a house and several covered bodies were lying there no doubt they had been in the basement of that house and died when it was hit by a bomb.

Somehow my mother got in touch with my father who came to see us but had to soon leave again. In the meantime, grandmother was moved to another hospital. We went to see her there and found out that her injuries were so severe that she had to stay in the hospital much longer than we thought. In the shelter, there were several other children my age and we played when we were not busy trying to find something to eat or getting water at the well. Then came the day when another air raid came and we ran to the shelter and remained there for many hours, only to emerge to a burning city again. But this time, as we approached the house where our room was, we saw nothing but a blazing inferno and again we were without shelter. Mother told me that we had to go to a public shelter and stay until something else could be found for us. The day finally arrived when father came with a truck and we got in and left.

Mother told me later that when father came to see us that first time, he told her that he would be back in a few days, maybe a week, and for us to be ready to leave as soon as he returned. He had found a place for us in the country about 50 miles away, where there were no factories or military targets for the American and British bombers. So, off we went into the country. It was so nice to see houses that were not damaged or destroyed and fields covered with snow that looked so clean and bright. Finally, we arrived at a farmhouse surrounded by trees and when we drove into the courtyard, I saw a stable with cows, some dogs and a cat and thought to myself that I should like it here. We were shown a room where another family from the city already lived and were told that we had to share two rooms with them. The other family's father was on the Russian Front and the lady had three children. They had come from another city where the bombings had left hardly any buildings where people could live. Father had to turn around and leave to get back to Kassel and we did not see him again for some time. I am not sure exactly how long it was before we saw him again.

So there we were in two rooms with four other people but it was so quiet there. The rooster crowed early in the morning and I was startled until I found out what was making the unfamiliar noise. The days were spent playing in the farmyard and in the barn, where we discovered some kittens and that kept us very busy for a while. Children do not always understand everything going on in the adult world and we did some things without asking the right or wrong of it. There was a very large chicken coop and we sneaked in and took the eggs out of the nests. Since I had the jacket with the hood, it was my job to carry the eggs and take them to our rooms, making sure no one saw what we did, especially the farmer and his family. As mother told me later, the farmer was forced to take in families from cities where there were heavy air raids and did not like it at all. They would not share food with us and we had to find what we could because the village with stores was a long way away. Even there, food was hard to find, since the whole country was almost destroyed!

The farmer also had a storage room with glass jars of fruit and vegetables and once we found that, we took some of those jars. Yes, we children learned to steal when we were hungry. (Note: Desperate times always cause desperate measures that would never be utilized by [illegible]ized people if conditions were normal. Eventually, after sufficient trauma, we all will revert to a survival mode. This behavior is seemingly built into our genes. In hindsight, one should not feel guilty for any non-violent survival behavior caused by the desperation of such times.)

So time went by and spring came, the most peaceful quiet time since leaving the city. Then one day father came to visit us again, as he had several times before, only this time he wore his Luftwaffe Uniform. As mother told me later, he was in a hurry to leave and did not have time to change and store his uniform in the vault (locker) where he usually put it before leaving the city. So here he was, sitting at the table with us, when a loud knock on the door startled us and when mother went to open it, a group of soldiers in different uniforms burst into the room. The soldiers shouted in a strange language and went toward my father and grabbed him. They had large guns and before I knew what happened, they were gone and Father with them. It was the American Army, on their way east, that took my father prisoner and also every other German in uniform.

The next day mother and I were walking to the village when the American officer that took my father prisoner the evening before drove by in a jeep. Mother spoke to him and asked him again, as she had the night before, if he could tell her where they were taking my father. He could only tell her that he really did not know. Then he asked my mother where her hometown was and when she said Kassel, he said it would be good for her to make her way there with me because the Russians were going to occupy the area where we were and the city of Kassel and surrounding areas would be under American occupation.

The allied powers had divided Germany and the Russians were going to get the eastern part and the Americans, British and French divided the western part. The border ran right in the middle of where we were. There were many refugees making their way west because no one wanted to fall into the hands of the Russians, since stories of their cruelty toward German civilians had preceded them. One day mothe[r] said to me that she had to go to Kassel to see about grandmother find a place for us to live since we could not live in Dingelstadt forever. I was to stay with the other lady and her children until she returned. So she set out with a bicycle and after many days reached Kassel. As she told me later another young woman went with her and they encountered many checkpoints, and were only allowed to pass when they explained, in English, why they were trying to get to Kassel. Americans at that time understood why no woman wanted to fall into Russians hands. As soon as mother arrived in Kassel she tried to find grandmother and a place to stay for a while. As she was walking on a sidewalk, pushing her bike, she met an Italian lady and her husband whom she had met in the same shelter we went to during the bombing of the city. They had exchanged food and services (he was a tailor). They were happy to meet again and after finding out mother had just arrived and needed a place to live, they took her to a house where they and many other families had found rooms. They had two daughters and my mother was put in a room with them and was very thankful to have a bed for the night.

Mother also had need of some new clothes and they were provided for her by her friends. It was the most joy my mother had in a long time and, as it turned out, a very fortunate meeting for the other family also. It was no easy task trying to find someone when the hospitals were a long distance to walk; then when mother got there she was told grandmother had been discharged several months ago and there was no forwarding address. But first she needed to go to the American Headquarters and register; everyone had to do so. Since she could speak fluent English, it was no problem to be understood.

Before the war, Mother was a secretary at the Henschel Werke, a defense plant in Kassel. In Germany and most of Europe, children are taught at least one other language besides their own. In my school, English and French were mandatory and later we also learned some Latin. So Mother registered and then went on her quest again, searching for grandmother. After an exhausting day of walking for ...s trying to get information on her whereabouts, she came back to ...m with the family and they all sat together planning what to do

on the next day. Some of them were looking for jobs, some for other friends lost during the war but most of all everyone was looking for food and other needed items.

Trading things for food was the most common way of procuring one's necessities in those days. Early the next morning, mother started out again on her daily quest for grandmother. Walking around in a city that had been over 75% destroyed was no easy task. There were the remnants of the bombed out houses spilled over into the street and great holes left by bombs which missed the houses. Unexploded ordinance was seen and heard to go off every day and people who had escaped the actual bombings were killed later.

In the meantime, I was in the eastern part of Germany and the Russian Army was fast advancing in my direction. The lady who kept me gave me food with the understanding that I would always get eggs from the henhouse and try to go to the farmer's kitchen to see if there was anything else I could get that was edible. Her own children did the same and so we had various things to eat and did not starve but I missed my mother terribly and asked about her often. The reply was always the same: "Your mother is gone and will never come back, who knows if she is even alive." So there I sat at the window, overlooking the farmyard, crying my heart out, hoping it was not true that my mother would not return to pick me up. Weeks and weeks went by and we, the other children and I, were busy climbing over fences into people's gardens to look for food. When we found fruit, we first ate all we could and then carried more home with us. Several times we were caught and severely reprimanded but it did not stop us; we were hungry and did what we were told. So time went by, my sitting at the window looking for my mother and the lady telling me how stupid I was to keep looking because that my mother would not return. But then one afternoon a strange looking vehicle (a jeep) drove into the farmyard; my mother jumped out, I ran as fast as I could toward her and we were together again. She was alive and did come back for me. Then I saw two men in the same uniform worn by the soldiers who picked up my father many months before, get out of the jeep and hand out candy to all the other children gathered around them. My mother just took my hand and led me to the jeep; we got in, the soldiers got in and away we went. I could scarcely believe it; here I was with my mother and we were leaving that place where I had grieved so and finally could not shed any more tears.

It was one of the most amazing things, here with those soldiers, who were smiling and giving me candy and talking in a language I did not understand; unlike the soldiers who had taken away my father and were not friendly. As we rode along, mother told me that she found grandmother and that we would live in a beautiful house and I would never have to go back to that farm. How was all that possible? As I heard from mother then and again later, when I understood all of the details, the following is what happened during the time mother left me at the farm.

After mother walked around the city again that day, she came back to the room she shared with the Italian lady's daughter. As soon as she arrived, mother's friends excitedly started telling her that an American jeep with two soldiers had come during the day looking for her. Did mother know why? The soldiers left word for my mother to stay there and that they were coming to pick her up in the morning. So, as promised, the soldiers came back the next morning and told mother that they had orders to bring her to the Headquarters Building where she had registered the day before. When she arrived, she was taken to the Commander's office and asked to sit down and then she heard the most wonderful question in a long time. Would she like to work for the American Army as an interpreter since her command of the English language was excellent and they needed her to talk to the many displaced persons and help in general with translating all the necessary paperwork? Of course, mother was overjoyed at the prospect but as she told me later, she did not express that right away. There were some things she had to take care of first before she could take the position and she explained what they were to the American Major.

She had to find a place to live, then locate her mother and then get her daughter from the east and that in a hurry because of the advancing Russian Army. No problem, he said. After filling out the necessary papers, she was taken home again in the jeep and told to be ready again first thing in the morning and then she would be picked up by the driver and brought back to Headquarters. So far, so good thought Mother. Sure enough, the next morning the jeep was back and Mother rode back to Headquarters. Then came the big surprise. The Major told mother that they were going to drive to a very nice part of town, not too far from Headquarters and she was to pick out a house. Yes, such was the power of the occupation forces! They drove to the area where there were nice two family houses with gardens and mother pointed to one she liked and they stopped. The American soldiers went to the door and explained to the bewildered homeowners that the American Forces needed the house and for them to make arrangements to move out.

When mother heard that, she translated all that to the owner. She asked the officer if it were possible that the owner could just move upstairs, since it was a separate apartment. Fine, he said, if she was okay with it. Certainly it was a better arrangement, mother told me later. The homeowner did as he was told and Mother moved in the next day. It was a very nice place to live in, a big kitchen, large living room, dining room, a large bathroom and three bedrooms. Then, with the help of the Americans, she was able to find Grandmother, who had moved in with friends, whose house had escaped destruction. Riding in a jeep was a lot faster than walking. Mother had to work for a while before arrangements were made to go and pick me up. She told me later of the great fear she had not being able to get to me before the Russians got there. So all was well, as much as it could be, in those tumultuous times.

We were on our way to Kassel and I looked forward to seeing my grandmother again and the knowledge of not having to run to the shelter anymore added greatly to my sense of wellbeing. In the meantime, mother also found out that my father was a POW in France and he could write letters to her. When he could return, no one knew. Now our lives took on a completely new dimension. Mother was picked up every morning by a driver in a jeep and sometimes there was another soldier with him. Both of them always had chocolate bars or chewing gum for the children who always gathered around any time Americans made an appearance. Needless to say, I was a popular girl then and enjoyed it so much. I started school and was so ready to go and learn and be around children my age and have lots of friends to play with. In the mornings, a group of us walked to school, which took about twenty minutes. When we arrived our teacher, Herr Basermann, met us at the door and greeted us by name; something I think now was very thoughtful. Our first lessons were written on little chalkboards with chalk pencils; it was in second grade that we received paper to write on. We also received care packages from America filled with good things to eat and a pair of loafers for me. I was so thrilled to have American shoes; even though they were a bit snug, I wore them anyway.

My friends and I would go to the main road that led to the center of Kassel, Frankfurter Strasse, and watch for the Americans to come by, which they did all day long. I had no idea that there were so many trucks in the world. We waved and they waved back and often threw chewing gum and chocolate to us. They were probably very happy someone gave them a friendly wave instead of shooting at them. Life was good in those first years after the war ended and my friends and I enjoyed doing some really fun things. One really good thing was that we had food to eat, something we often lacked during the war years. And it was quiet, no more running to the shelter and hoping the bombs would miss us while we were running.

In front of our house, across the street, was a field where the farmers planted potatoes and when the harvest came around, all of us children were allowed to follow the farm workers and gather the small potatoes they left behind. My grandmother was very happy about it, since even potatoes were rationed. On other fields were sugar beets, a highly valued commodity because of the sweetness of the cooked, finished product, sugar beet syrup; what a treat to eat that on a piece of buttered bread!

After the harvest, when snow covered the fields, we put on our snow skis and went all across those fields toward a little hill and that's when the fun really began. On the side of that hill we built little ramps and then started higher up the hill so that we would gather some speed and then jump from those ramps. Oh, what a great time we had there! Other times, we would tie four or five our sleds together and then everyone got on, and down the hill we would go at a pretty high speed. We stayed out until late at night, it was light with the moon in the night sky and it was cold. But did we care? No, even though our feet were ice cold, our mittens stiff with ice and our noses red. Many times there were high snowdrifts in front of the area where the fields began and we jumped in them and disappeared. Great fun! Also, when the snowy roads melted a little and then froze again at night it provided us with a ready-made surface we could ice skate on. That was the time when one of the officers mother worked for gave her a doll for me since he had heard about the time when all our things were burned. Americans seemed to be the kindest people I had ever met. One thing I wanted most was to learn to understand the strange language the American soldiers spoke. We picked up a word here and there, as children do, but to really speak it was something that would take a lot of practice and many more years of learning. Sometimes I was allowed to go to the place where mother worked.

Before the war, the large house, called a Villa in German, had belonged to a wealthy family, but when the Americans needed a place for their offices they took the Villa and made it in to one of their many administration buildings. There was a beautiful terrace out back and on a trellis some grapes were growing. A large garden was also there and I enjoyed playing in it. It was there that I ate my first peanut butter and jelly sandwich on white bread. Such a very strange kind of bread, I thought, so white and soft; it stuck to the roof of my mouth along with the peanut butter. But I liked it then and still do now. Mother was able to bring home many food items that were impossible to find on the

German market. Real coffee was practically unobtainable, unless it could be found on the black market for a great amount of money or a valuable item one could trade. But we had coffee and many other good things to eat, thanks to the generosity of the Americans where mother worked.

Mother translated letters for some soldiers and they gave her American cigarettes, which were worth a fortune on the black market. Food in the German grocery stores was rationed and many items were not available at all. We had many good food items available and I was introduced to American sandwiches, also, cake with frosting so different from the way German cakes are made. I got my first orange and bit into it not knowing it had to be peeled first. One time, mother brought an American magazine home, The Saturday Evening Post, and it quickly became my favorite. The pictures in it showed beautifully dressed people, especially girls who wore dresses I really liked but had never seen before. Also, I remember seeing advertisements for milk with Elsie the cow and thought it most funny. Pictures in that magazine became my dream world; all the things I saw were things I wanted to have one day. Slowly I began to pick up some American words here and there and was able to make out what the words meant in the magazine. My mother helped a lot. Then I found the American radio station, AFN, and began listening to the music and really liked it and do so to this day. Of course it was the music of the 40's.

My Uncle Helmut returned from a POW camp six months after the war ended and lived with us. How happy my grandmother was to have her son home after not seeing him for years. Uncle Helmut had been shot down twice with his plane but escaped both times when he parachuted safely to the ground. Not very long after he came home, I walked into our bathroom and was startled by what was in the bathtub, a very large hog, dead of course. Uncle Helmut had begun what was to be a very successful business, trading on the black market. That night, after all the necessary items were assembled, the work of putting as much of that hog as possible into jars began. We ate very well for a long time afterward. There also was a vegetable garden in the back yard and lots of things grew there; carrots, cabbage, lettuce, potatoes and also dill and borage, herbs needed to make green sauce which is sour cream with hard boiled eggs and then eaten over hot potatoes.

We had a cherry tree and plum tree and I was able to climb into those anytime I wanted without fear of being caught doing something wrong. Time went by quickly and one day, almost a year after the war ended, as I arrived home from school, I first went into the back yard for something and saw the silhouette of a man leaning against the kitchen window. It was not Uncle Helmut, I knew, but who could it be? I went into the house and toward the kitchen to find out; when my grandmother met me and said, "come and see your father, he has just returned!" How strange, I thought, he does not look much like he used to look, the way I remembered him in his uniform with all those ribbons. He had also lost a lot of weight. But I was happy to see him and for along time we talked about all the things I was doing and how we all were so happy the war was finally over. Later I noticed the cane he used when walking. He had been injured in the last few days of the war and that injury gave him trouble as long as he lived. Everyone was happy to see him, especially Uncle Helmut; now he had a partner for The Business. Yes, he and father really got busy and started doing business in a big way. In the meantime, uncle had become friendly with a young lady whose father owned a flour mill. He was, therefore, able to get flour, a very much sought after commodity, and trade it for other items needed by the people.

So a truck was obtained and loaded with flour sacks and I sat on top of them with another much valued item tied around my waist, hidden under my coat; American cigarettes.

So off we went to trade for household items, such as brooms, brushes and mops and also much needed luxury items including leather purses, billfolds and suitcases and a host of other things people needed. After obtaining all the goods, we drove back to Kassel where a large table was set up on the market place and everything was quickly sold. Then the same routine started again and so it went for a few years, until the time came that my father decided to go into business for himself in his hometown of Essen. I was not very happy about that at all because I had to leave the life I enjoyed so much and had gotten used to and worse of all, I had to leave my grandmother. Here ended one of the most carefree times of my life and nothing ever came close to the happy times I spent in Kassel after the war, there in that house the Americans got for us. Grandmother and Uncle Helmut moved to a house not far away from the one we had lived in and mother and father and I moved to Essen.

My father's parents had died earlier in the year and I was sad that I never really got to know them. My parents had gone to the funeral alone and it was then that father decided to go into business in Essen. People needed coal and my father bought a fleet of trucks to transport that coal to businesses and so he became the sole provider for our little family again. The city of Essen was also very much in ruins and the apartment we went to had belonged to the grandparents. The building had taken a hit from a bomb but only half the building collapsed and since there had not been a fire, the rest stayed somewhat intact. I say somewhat because the staircase was open on one side and only covered by flimsy materials which let cold air flow freely. The staircase was not stable and I always dreaded venturing up to the second floor to the apartment. It was also the last floor still standing in a house that originally had four floors. The ceilings were not in good condition, with cracks in them where sometimes sand rained down on us. But with so many houses destroyed and so many people looking for just about anything to live in, we were fortunate to have what we did and so made the best of it.

This area had once been very nice and the houses had been stately, solidly built apartment houses. Now almost every other house and, sometimes, whole blocks were a pile of rubble and most of the tall trees had also been destroyed, so it was a very bleak place to live. But it was like that all over the city and people were happy to have a roof over their heads and no more air raids and no bombs falling and being in constant danger of getting killed. But my world was not the same anymore and I grieved for my grandmother, Kassel and the life I had to leave behind. The school I attended was a Catholic Convent School for girls only. The nuns who were our teachers were very kind and I loved going there every day. We had classes in English, French and Latin and lots of history. My favorite was English and my grades were excellent in that subject. We also had a class in sewing and embroidery where we were taught very useful things that I still do today. My one favorite item was a blue linen apron embroidered with blue and yellow threads and it hangs in my kitchen today. Knitting and crocheting were also taught and there we knitted a red and grey striped sweater, which was worn for many years. The no nonsense attitude of the nuns contributed a great deal to our ability to learn and retain much of what was taught and I know that it was the reason I developed a love for learning more. Now I could listen to the English language radio stations and my favorite music and actually understand lots of the words. My other hobby was reading. I read many books about America and especially about the early discovery of that land I admired so much. There were books in the library that told about the South and the plantations, the cotton fields, the river boats, the lush vegetation and I became a steady patron. Flowers and trees I had never heard of, much less seen, grew there and the climate was warm, much warmer than in Germany. My insatiable hunger was satisfied with every word, but I always found more books that opened up a new perspective of America and also of other countries I read about. So very fascinating were the ancient Egyptians and the English Kings and Queens that I soon became a real book worm.

My social life was not very good, there were some children in the neighborhood and we played in the ruins of the bombed out houses, building forts, playing hide and seek and throwing rocks through the empty windows that were in some of the brick walls that still stood. Many of those walls crumbled into large heaps at times and it was only because of God's providence that we were not covered with all that debris. When it rained, we made little dams with sand and rocks and made ships out of newspaper and other light materials.

All these years I had wished for a brother or sister and never got one and now that I was ten years old my mother announced one day that I was indeed going to get a brother or a sister. Of course I was very happy and looked forward to the day, which was going to be in late December of 1949. I helped mother all I could with the laundry since we had no washing machine and I would carry the wet clothes outside and put them on the clothesline. Sometimes the weather was really bad, and then we hung the clothes on a little balcony. Then, when it was really cold, the clothes had to be dried inside which was even harder because there was no bathtub where they could drip. But somehow things got done. We had a large zinc bathtub and our baths in it were spaced several days apart since it meant heating water on the coal stove and later emptying the tub, a chore no one liked.

Then on the 24th of December 1949, my bother Joachim was born. Oh, how happy I was to have a baby brother and I could not hold him enough or help enough to dress or undress him for his bath. Spring came and the weather was warmer and father had bought the most beautiful baby buggy in the whole world, mother and I thought. "Nothing is too good for my son", father would say. So we wrapped Joachim up and I walked him around the neighborhood in his buggy and it was duly admired by all who saw it. Eleven year old girls love babies and some of the girls my age that lived nearby also had siblings they were allowed to walk about. So when the weather was good, we were sometimes three or four girls pushing buggies and strollers with babies or small children.

Summer came and I was allowed to go to the swimming pool at a lake on the outskirts of town. Several of us went together and rode the streetcar to the pool. It did not happen very often, as little money was available for these things. Later that same year, in the fall, mother and I were able to buy me a new dress and coat and hat. How proud I was to get something new. I had grown quite a bit and needed lots of new things but some things just had to wait until more money was available. So life went on and Joachim was one year old at Christmas; we celebrated his birthday and Christmas together. After the weather became warmer, I played with my friends in the ruins again and we started to build a really large fort, as we called it. We got the word "fort" from the American Westerns we watched sometimes in the movie theater. So we were busy throwing large boulders to each other to stack up, that when I bent down, one of those boulders hit me on my forehead. I put my hand on my head and right away I saw blood running down the sleeve of my blue sweater. I ran home as fast as I could and when mother saw me she fainted and a neighbor, who saw me running, was right behind me and helped my mother. Then we took Joachim and ran to the doctor's office around the corner who then took care of me. It turned out to be a very deep cut and bled profusely but a large bandage took care of it. The scar is still on my forehead. When we arrived home again, mother told me the reason she fainted must have been because of all that blood and possibly because she was pregnant again.

In September, Ralf was born and, of course, I was happy to have another brother. Joachim was a cute little toddler at that time and was very interested in his new little brother. We washed, I hung the clothes out, I went shopping, helped mother clean house, went to school and took Joachim out to play. So life continued for another year when, one day, mother said that we were moving to another apartment. That was great news for all of us and I could not wait for that day to arrive. Then one day we moved way to the other side of town to a newly built apartment house on the third floor. It had two bedrooms, a living room, kitchen and bath. Finally we had a bathtub! The hot water did not have to be heated on the stove. Mother bought new furniture for the living room, for the bedrooms and the kitchen and we even had a refrigerator. Life was good again. But those were only the outside things one can enjoy along with peace and quiet. The one girl I became friendly with lived a few houses away and was about two years older and had a boyfriend who worked in a coal mine. Mother told me right then not to entertain any thoughts of having a boyfriend, besides I was too busy with school and work at home to have time for anything like that. There were no social activities or after school events I was able to attend and so my life became more and more involved with books and the dream castles I would build after reading a particularly interesting book.

This was the time when I remembered the American magazines I used to look at while living in Kassel and all the pictures of pretty things in them. I wished I had them now because I would be able to read the stories in them now that my command of the English language had been greatly improved. But I did listen to the radio and was familiar with all the popular music of the day, as were many German teens at that time. It seemed that everything American was popular. During that time, there was not much in Germany to be excited about for teens and so the new things from America were much sought after.

Then came the month of February 1955 and a great event changed our lives again. Father went to work in the mornings and sometimes came home in the evenings and sometimes not. I remember my mother telling him if he was not careful and drank too much he would have an accident and possibly die. One morning he got ready to go to work dressed in his suit and tie, hat and black leather coat, his briefcase in hand and he walked out. When he did not come home we all went to bed only to be awakened several hours later by the doorbell. There stood a policeman who told my mother that there had been an accident and she should go to the hospital right away. She woke me and told me and then she went into the night, walking to the streetcar stop and getting to the hospital as fast as she could. Today we wonder why the police did not drive her but back then the policeman who came rode his bicycle. The next morning mother came home and I could tell the news was not good. Our father was dead. He had been in a streetcar on his way home and as the streetcar turned a corner my father, who leaned against the door, fell out when the door opened.

He had been drinking and therefore no compensation was given to my mother. We were really poor then. At the funeral there was only a preacher and my mother and I. It was a very cold winter and snow was on the ground. Mother had to find a job, which she did. She started selling vacuum cleaners door to door but that did not last long and she looked for something else. All this time I stayed home and kept Joachim and Ralf, cooked and washed clothes and cleaned. The boys liked to go outside in the snow and ride the sled and have me pull them around. Then in the summer, the boys and I went to Kassel to visit our grandmother to stay a few weeks. My friend Edith had a date with an American and she asked him if he could bring another GI and the four of us could go out dancing.

And so we did. It sure was fun then to go somewhere with other people and have a good time. Now as I think back, I cannot even remember his name. After that first date, we all decided to go to the service club for the next date and so we did. We ate hamburgers and drank Coke, a great new experience. Real American hamburgers, we were impressed. Dancing was my passion and I enjoyed it very much. So for a few weeks I enjoyed life as never before. One evening as I was dancing with what-ever-his name was; I noticed one of the soldiers looking at me constantly. Then as we walked off the dance floor, the guy was leaning against the bar and he looked at me and winked. When we got back to our table, I asked who that was and they said: "That's old Mefford". Oh, I said, how old is he? About 22, they said. Well, he sure was old in my thinking, since I was only 16. So the next week I had a date again to go to the movies with my American friend and I was to come to the Kaserne and he would meet me at the gate. So when I got there and told the gate guard who I was waiting for, he told me that that guy had been sent to Frankfurt that day and would not return until tomorrow. As soon as he had finished telling me the sad tale, I noticed old Mefford walking toward the gate and when he got close he started telling me that same story about the guy who was sent to Frankfurt. But he continued, immediately asking if I would go to the movie with him. Well, even though he was pretty old, going to the movie with him would sure beat walking home again and doing nothing. So we went in and he bought popcorn and coke and we saw The Three Stooges and another movie I do not remember. Later, as we were walking home, I found out that his name was Bobby and that his home state was Alabama. He asked me how old I was and I lied and said 18. He did not question it and so all was well. We made a date for the next day to go to the 1955 Garden Show in Kassel. There was just one problem; my two little brothers had to go with me since my grandmother was not able to keep them during the day. Joachim was five and Ralf was three. OK, he said, and so we met the next day and had a wonderful time at the garden show, where Bobby bought ice cream for the boys and me and we just walked around for several hours. Then, before I had to go home, Bobby asked me if I could meet him again that evening. I was really surprised because I did not expect another date with him. Yes, I said, after I put the boys to bed I would meet him. And so it went for a couple of weeks, we would meet and go to the Gasthaus or a movie or just walk around town and talk. I asked a lot of questions about his family and the town he was from and I got the answers to what I asked, no more and no less. There was a small park close to my home and we would sit on the one bench, waiting until it was time for him to leave and make bed check by midnight.

One evening after we knew each other for two weeks, we stopped under a street light on the way home. Then, to my surprise, Bobby asked me if I would marry him. I was stunned! He was a very nice guy and I liked him a lot, but marry him already? He then proceeded to tell me that he had only a few months left on his tour in Germany and he would soon go back to America. But if I would say I would marry him then he could re-enlist, go home on leave, then return to Germany and we could be married. Then came the time for me to tell him that I was only 16 until September and he said that it would not make any difference.

Well, I had to think fast. Here was a handsome American GI who wanted to marry me, and in my sixteen year old mind it was a really great thing, too good to pass up. Since I so loved everything American, and in my heart I knew that someday I wanted to marry one; I just did not think it would be this soon when someone would be serious. So the answer was yes. But I had to tell Bobby to write to my mother first and ask if she would give her consent to the marriage, since I was only 16. My mother arrived a few days later and after she met Bobby she told him she could not give her consent until I was at least 18. That was fine with him he said and we proceeded to buy the engagement rings. When we arrived late at the jewelry store and found it was already closed, we were very disappointed. But the owner was doing some rearranging in the show window and as we stood there looking he motioned for us to come to the door and when he opened it we told him what we wanted and he let us in. In Germany, the custom was to wear a gold band on the left hand ring finger until the wedding, when it would be switched to the right ring finger. There was no diamond engagement ring, but who cared? Not I.

I was happy with the ring that had the engagement date, September 10, 1955 and his name in it and I was wearing it proudly. We were engaged and then I had to leave to go back to Essen with my brothers. Bobby promised to write to me while he was in the States and then as soon as he returned we would start putting our papers in to get married. We knew from other couples all about the paper war that was awaiting us and the many months it would take to finally get approved by the US Army for marriage. After we arrived in Essen, the time went by so very slow until I received my first letter from Bobby. Until then, I wanted to believe with all my heart he would not be one of those soldiers we heard about that said they would come back to Germany and get married, but then never did. He wrote many letters while on the boat going to America and then when he arrived in Huntsville he continued writing and sending me packages. One gift in particular was so wonderful; a pink sweater set that was all the rage at the time. And it coming from America made it all the more special. We were not to see each other again until the next year when he came to Essen to visit for a few days. Then it was summer, when I took the boys for a visit to grandmother's again, before Bobby and I would be able to spend time together.

We worked on getting our papers together, but I do not think we were very serious at times because we knew my mother would not sign the papers until I was 18. But then living in a different town and only visiting occasionally was not good. Finally, in early 1957, mother and the boys and I moved to Kassel and then things began to move right along. Our papers were ready and we were married. Bobby had one friend along and there was mother, grandmother, Joachim and Ralf. A very small wedding party indeed who went to lunch at a nearby restaurant and then home where there were strawberry pies and other goodies. Ralf and Joachim had their first whole bottle of Coca Cola and were very satisfied with that. Later in the afternoon, Bobby and I and Daugherty went to the service club where we continued to celebrate with our friends. We had already rented a room where we would live and all our meager possessions were already there when we arrived later that night. And so we were married and life was good, until Saturday when Bobby had to go to the field for the weekend. It was a short honeymoon indeed. The next significant event was the birth of our first baby, Susan Lynn.

Return to Germany

Now we are finally back in Germany, after four years of not seeing or speaking to my mother and two brothers. My mother did not have a phone and if they had, I had no money to make a transatlantic phone call to Germany. Bobby was waiting at the Rhein - Main airport and we drove right to Kassel to see my family. Oh, how happy I was to see them again and to show off my two pretty girls, who were then four and three years old. And then came all the good eating I had missed, and the good bread and just being home again.

My mother had married again and her new husband was very nice! He took Susie and Nancy across the street and bought candy for them and was full of surprises. One day he came home from work and brought little spoon, knife and fork sets with the girl's names engraved on them. He said he noticed that their little hands were too small to handle the larger utensils and so he bought small ones for them. Since we had an American station wagon, my brothers were thrilled when I drove them to school, something they had never done. And of course their friends were duly impressed. Those few days went by too fast but Bobby had to go back to work and I wanted to get to my new quarters. They turned out to be on the third floor in the American Housing Area in Karlsruhe, in southern Germany. It would be a four hour drive to Kassel but with my good car and no speed limit on the autobahn; I looked forward to the first trip I would take there.

Life in Karlsruhe was good; Bobby's work was outside of town, about a thirty minute drive. Whenever I wanted the car, I would drive him to work or he would get a ride with someone and I could then go wherever I needed to go. There was a real nice zoo in Karlsruhe and we bought a season pass and went there often, since there was a big playground and a little lake with boats one could rent. Just as we went there the first time, a little (big) hippopotamus had been born and it was so cute. Then there was a newborn giraffe and a little enclosure with small houses where guinea pigs lived. As I recall, that was the favorite of most children, including mine. Susie and Nancy also loved riding in the streetcars, a new experience for children from Alabama who had never seen a streetcar before.

Not far away from Karlsruhe was a fairy tale castle with statues all throughout the grounds, which depicted the favorite German Grimm's fairy tales. In the housing area we had many good surprises and the favorite one was that on certain days of the week a German lady, with a station wagon, drove though the area with fresh cakes and bread and Brötchen, the little rolls so popular not only with Germans, but also many Americans. She would toot her car horn and lots of people poured out of the buildings to get to the 'Brötchen Lady', as she was affectionately called. Oh, how we loved her good fresh plum cakes, the good bread I had not eaten for so long and lots of other delicacies, too numerous to mention.

There was never a shortage of children to play with and there were sandboxes so favored by children (and cats too). In the winter, we had lots of snow and Susie and Nancy had snowsuits and a sled and enjoyed playing outside since they had never seen snow before. The

PX, the post exchange, and commissary were within walking distance and there was a unique service. The commissary had baggers and also drivers who would drive your groceries home, if you did not have transportation available.

We took several trips to Kassel and my mother and my brothers, Joachim and Ralf, came to visit us in Karlsruhe. They loved the American ice cream and the different food I cooked. Even though they never warmed up to cornbread, they both loved peanut butter and I would send them that for many years until it became available in Germany. Then came the day, in the spring of 1963, when Bobby came home on a Wednesday afternoon complaining of chest pains after a rough game of football. Yes, he played football and was good at it. He had been to the dispensary and the doctor there told him to wrap an ace bandage around his chest. A fellow player had run into Bobby's chest and caused a very serious injury, as we were about to find out several days later. On the following Sunday, Bobby's whole company went to bridge training near Heidelberg. At noon, as he recalls, he went to get his lunch when a sharp pain hit him on the left side up to his shoulder and he passed out. Being close to Heidelberg, with a military hospital, he was transported there immediately. After evaluation, the doctor called me in Karlsruhe and told me to rush up there to the hospital as quick as I could, he gave my husband a slim chance to survive.

Well, I rushed to find a friend who could keep the girls and it was her husband who drove me there, about thirty miles on the autobahn. When I arrived, Bobby was still in the operating room and so we waited and waited until several hours later the surgeon came out and talked to me. My husband had maybe a fifty/ fifty chance of survival, since at the time of the injury on Wednesday he had been bleeding internally because of a ruptured spleen. I believe I was in such shock I could not stand and almost fainted. The thought of him dying was not anything I had ever imagined and not being a Christian at that time I did not even know how to pray. So I waited until I could go to see him and was so overwhelmed at the sight of him hooked up to so many tubes and just lying there not moving but breathing!

After a while, we drove back to Karlsruhe and I collected the girls and went to our apartment in the next stairwell. It was so hard to explain the truth to them but told them that the next day I had to go back and visit daddy and they could not go until another day. So they went to my friend again and I drove to the hospital to see Bobby. What a pitiful sight to see my husband lying there helpless, not able to do much of anything but just lie there. He stayed in the hospital for about a week as I recall and improved daily until the doctor could say for sure that he would live. All that time I made trips to the hospital as much as I could and somewhere the girls must have heard me say that their daddy almost died. On the day he came home we walked into the living room and Susie asked, "Are you going to die now daddy?"

The recovery was slow and Bobby was put on special duty after he was released from medical care. That duty consisted of working at the AYA, the youth services in the housing area. Once a year there was a carnival close by the housing area and the commissary had a stand there where they sold little packages of ice cream: vanilla, chocolate and strawberry. The German people loved those and Bobby came home at night with a large amount of cash, in the thousands, just for selling ice cream. So he spent almost a year on special duty before going back to his regular job.

Then on the 13th of August, 1964, we welcomed Karen Ann into our family, how beautiful she was with black hair and brown eyes and so cuddly and chubby. I had a German bassinette for her and sometimes Susie and Nancy thought it great fun when we put her into one of their doll buggies. A little new baby is the most wonderful thing in the world and I never cease to marvel at how much I can love a baby. We knew then that in October we had to return to the states and Karen being still small, I wanted to buy a little carry-bed for her and I found one in town.

Then came the day in October when we had to leave again and say goodbye to my family. It was so hard to leave and to know my mother would not see her grandchildren again for many years. We moved to Ft. Campbell, Kentucky, and lived there from October 1964 until early 1966, when Bobby came home one day telling me he had orders to go to Viet Nam. I had expected those orders because the war had been going on for a while and many other soldiers, who were our neighbors, had been deployed. So, back to Huntsville for us and into our own apartment around the corner from my mother-in-law Ruby. She was happy to have her grandchildren so close. Then after 13 month's Bobby came home and we moved to Ft. Benning.

There the great change came into my life, in the form of some ladies visiting from a Baptist church and inviting me. I was very rude the first time they came and slammed the door after telling them I was Catholic. Which was true, but in reality I was a lost person, not going to church and not caring at all about God. But they came back and one lady talked with me and told me about how Jesus died for me and gave me something to read which I now know to be the Romans Road. As I read that, something stirred in me as if a sharp pain went through my chest and I thought to myself "That is me" and from that time on I thought about what that might have meant, since I never experienced anything like it before.

Then the ladies came back and told me about Vacation Bible School (VBS) and, of course, I was curious, since I never heard that term before. So when the time came for VBS to start I took Susie, Nancy and Karen and went. It was very nice and the girls enjoyed it. After that, we went to church a few times but nothing significant happened that I can remember. Then one day, in the fall, Bobby came home with the usual papers in hand that ordered him to Korea. So we prepared for the move again back to Huntsville. But this time we started looking for a house to buy and after looking a few days, we found what we could afford and bought it and Bobby left.

That was February 1968. A few days after he left, the North Koreans hijacked an American ship, the Pueblo, and for a while we thought there might be another war starting. But all was resolved and it was peace after all. We started attending Meadow Hills Baptist Church, where Mary, Bobby's sister, was a member. And there I heard for the first time in my life that Jesus died for me, Margret Mefford, personally, and that I was a sinner and all the good things I did could not get me to heaven. Well, that message did not sit right with me at all. Me, a sinner? Up to that time, the word sinner really was not in my vocabulary and I pictured some sloppy, dirty, longhaired, unkempt creature in association with that word. But I kept on going to church and also to the "Good News Club" on Thursday afternoon with the children. There I watched the story of Esther on a flannel-graph and it intrigued me to no end. Also, the missionary stories really appealed to me and I got a good picture what real Christianity was all about. After several weeks of hearing the preaching and teaching, I began to realize that yes, all of mankind are sinners and I was indeed a sinner and only Jesus could save me. That is when I told Him that I believed that He did indeed die for me and would He please save me. And I know He did. My zeal for learning all I could about Him and all things in the Bible became a driving force in my life and I read as much as possible and asked many questions. Of course, the terminology was new and a dictionary was always present. That whole year was the most memorable of my life because my real life began then.

When Bobby came back in March, we moved to Fort Gordon, GA. We stayed in Huntsville so Susie and Nancy could finish school in May and then we would move also. But while Bobby was in Fort Gordon, he received orders to go to West Point, New York. So he arranged to rent an apartment for the summer and we would join him there. He came to Huntsville to pick us up and we went to West Point for the summer. It is a beautiful place and we all loved it. We took a river cruise up the Hudson River and back. The museum there is outstanding with many German war relics and also the grave of General George Custer at the graveyard.

In the meantime, I was pregnant with Linda. The day came for our departure in August and we went to Huntsville, then to Fort Gordon in September for the start of school. Our house was surrounded with lots of sand and I do not remember much grass. Linda was born on the second of January. The day before, New Years Day, I knew I had to go sometime in the evening and Bobby told me he would take me as soon as one of the football bowl games was finished. Well, it was at about 11 pm when we left. I had gotten the girls ready and they had their new housecoats and nightgowns on that they received at Christmas. So we piled into the station wagon and Bobby took me to the Hospital and then went home again with the girls. Linda was born a little after 6 a.m. on the second of January. She had a head full of black hair and was so chubby and cuddly and again we all just marveled at how much we loved our new little girl. They came to see me and then I saw them again when Bobby picked Linda and me up on the third day and we went home. We never had any idea how long we would live anywhere and sure enough on the 7th of February we moved again, this time back to Fort Benning, Georgia. I did not unpack everything this time and just got the necessary items out. A month or so later, Bobby said that he had orders to go to Germany. Oh boy, was I happy! Until I heard that he would go first and we would follow later. How much later we did not know. So back to Huntsville with four children to search for a furnished apartment and the knowledge that I might get orders any day to move to Germany.

Well, I found one and we received our orders in August of 1970, then we were on our way. Bobby met us in Frankfurt and we went to visit my family right away. I was so proud to show off our girls and see my mother and brothers again. We were stationed in Karlsruhe, just a block away from where we lived in 1962-64, when Karen was born.

Then a surprise, I was pregnant with Kevin and he arrived on the 1st of June in 1971 in Heidelberg. After four girls, I was so surprised to have a boy and of course thankful he was healthy. He did not have as much hair as the girls but then a boy gets a short haircut anyway as soon as needed. He was very long and slender and all the girls just wanted to hold him. We put him in Karen's doll buggy and rode him around in the apartment. When I put him in the playpen, in his little seat, I also had to put mosquito netting all over it because Linda always wanted to give him things like cookies and toys.

We left Germany in August 1972, just the children and me, since they had to start school and we did not want to move again in the middle of a school year. The trip was torture, I did not sleep for about 24 hours and we finally arrived in Huntsville after three plane changes. Bobby came home in the spring of 1973 and was stationed in Fort Campbell, KY. We decided that since it would not be long before he would have his twenty years in, we would stay in the house in Huntsville and he would come home on weekends. The children were happy that we were settled and so was I. New furniture was bought and we began to put down roots again, this time for good, or so I thought. We went back to Meadow Hills Baptist Church where the girls were in the youth group and started to make new friends and they went to their respective schools, two different ones to be exact. Susie and Nancy went to Johnson High, Karen went to West Mastin Lake Elementary School and Kevin and Linda were not of school age yet. Things went wonderfully for a while, Bobby came home on Friday evenings and like clockwork he came down the street a little after 8 pm, as I remember. The children would wait on the porch for him and talked about who would see him first.

One Friday evening, Bobby came home as usual and all was well until the next day when he told me that he had re-enlisted. What a bombshell! It meant moving again and finding someone to rent the house for several years. And leaving the wonderful church and my friends again was not something I got very excited about. In other words, I was not a happy person. But that was our life and Bobby was the one making the money and it was his career, so we did the necessary thing and moved to Fort Campbell, Kentucky. The first evening in our new quarters there was a thunderstorm and all the electricity went off. Our neighbor came over with candles and right away we realized we came from the same country. We were friends for the next nine months, when Bobby came home one day with new orders. This time it was to Fort Leonard Wood, Missouri.

Well, we were going west this time. When we arrived we were pleasantly surprised when we saw our new quarters. They had just been refinished and a new room with bath added on and the most beautiful hardwood floors. Susie, Nancy and Karen started school and in the fall Linda started Kindergarten and Kevin stayed home another year. One day, as I read the little newspaper (we received one a week), I came across an ad that said that if someone would like to start an Independent Church to call this number. Then later that evening, when Bobby came home, he told me that he heard on the radio where some people wanted to start an Independent Church. We called the number right away and met several like-minded couples later that week. Five military families started that Church, Maranatha Baptist Church, which is still there. Our piano was moved to a building that we found right outside the gate on The Spur toward St. Roberts. Then we called a pastor, who came from Alabama with his family.

And we grew and grew and many people were saved and then in the summer they were baptized in the Roubidoux River, which is very shallow. There we had many wonderful picnics and the children could play in the water and on the sandbanks. Our tour was three years and the longest ever in one place. So when Bobby decided to retire in 1978, I was very happy. And that is just what we did and moved back to Huntsville, where we lived for fifteen years before moving to East Limestone County, our current home.

Fifty years have now passed and we celebrated with children, grandchildren and great-grandchildren. They all came to help us celebrate that day and brought our three great-grandchildren. It really was a great surprise since we did not think several of the grandchildren could come. And how happy we were to see our children and grandchildren honor us in such a way. We love them all so very much and are very happy to live in this great country. Since beginning to write this chapter, my grandchildren have added six healthy, new great-grandchildren to the family and we thank God for them.

Chapter 3
ANNELIESE

Unhappy Childhood

I was born in Leipzig, Gohlis, Germany in 1926 and had one sister and one brother. My sister's name was Eva and my brother's name was Ralf. Sometime in the 1930s my parents divorced and my father married again. My mother moved to Kassel, where all her relatives lived. The step mother treated me and my sister Eva very badly. We were frequently beaten and denied food for the smallest infractions. (Editor's note: Anneliese does not know whether or not her mother had a job in Kassel. All she can remember is that her mother left, went to Kassel and Anneliese and her sister remained with their father and at the mercies of a most dysfunctional, spiteful and mean spirited stepmother. Incongruously, throughout all this, their father made no efforts to intervene in behalf of his daughters. Because of their tender age, the lack of intervention by their father made the experience more painful. Her mother was living with family relatives in Kassel during this sad and painful time in her life. Anneliese does not remember if her grandmother, who lived across the street, tried to mitigate their circumstances or not; but she does remember that her grandmother tried to give them food whenever she could. Anneliese, also does not know if her mother knew of their hellish plight. She suspects that she did not because of the strained relationship between her mother and her father and the lack of communication between them).

Why we (Anneliese and sister) could not go with mother to Kassel, I do not know, but it turned out to be an unbearable life with our father and stepmother. When one reads about stepmothers in the fairy tales we knew, they were always mean and treated the new children very badly. And so it was with our stepmother; she would beat us severely. I can never remember her being kind to us. When she had another baby with my father, this child could do no wrong and we were continually blamed for a lot of things that he did. When the new child broke something, or spilled anything, we girls were punished with severe beatings. Additionally, the stepmother would not provide adequate food for us. We were always hungry. We went to our grandmother's house whenever we could, to try to get milk, bread and any other food for ourselves. We had a little garden behind the apartment where we tried to raise vegetables to alleviate the hunger. And so our life went on, year after year. Only going to school was a diversion for us and a time to be free of our stepmother's evil presence.

Our grandmother's house was across the street from our house and that was another refuge for us besides school. Grandmother loved us and did what she could to make our lives more bearable. As an adult, it has always been a mystery to me why my father permitted the bad treatment that my sister and I suffered at the hands of this dysfunctional stepmother. I can only assume that either he did not know of it, (but I strongly suspect that he did), or was unable to confront her and insist that she provide the care that we needed as young children. Perhaps his personality was such that he just was unable to confront his new wife and endure the stressful scene that he knew would result.

Escape from Stepmother

When I was 14, I finished school and went for one year to a home as a household helper, where I learned all about the home, and in my case, this was also a store. This was a mandatory duty for all girls who finished school at 14, which was the age when one finished eight years of school. In Germany one starts school at six and goes eight years and then to a business school for practical training for office work or boys go to school or training for mechanic or something similar. The other career track is four years elementary school and then to a gymnasium which is a higher learning facility, equivalent to a high school in the U.S. From the gymnasium the goal is to go to a university after finishing thirteen years of school. At the time, this was the accepted school system in Germany.

The family I lived with during the day had a grocery store and one of my duties was to go to the market early with a pull wagon to buy fresh vegetables and fruit and bring them back to the store. We lived in the old town and the market was not far from the store. The one splendid thing about this arrangement was that I was away from the wicked and dysfunctional stepmother. When my year was over, I finally was able to leave and go to Kassel where my mother lived.

My sister Eva, also, went with me but our brother Ralf stayed with our father and stepmother. By this time our mother had married again. Her new husband was a very nice man who let us know that he loved us by treating us so very well. We learned to love him and to know what a happy family was like. After arriving in Kassel, I learned how to type and went to work at Henschel, a large industrial manufacturing complex where many things were made to support the war effort.

Wartime

When the bombing began to be intense, we had to go to the shelter often. We usually went to our basement shelter when there was an air raid alarm. Grandfather had built some wooden shelves there for the storage of potatoes and onions and canned items we had saved. He also put a rope between the shelves and we hung our clothes there so we would have something to wear when we stayed in the shelter for a longer time. He put a tub under the clothes and said that if we ever had to leave in a hurry we could just cut the rope and the clothes would fall into the tub and we could carry them out. But the situation proved to be different from what he expected. The men also made holes through the wall leading to the basement in the next house so that in case our house was hit and a fire broke out, we would then be able to escape to the other house and hopefully be safe.

Then there came that awful night of the worst air raid we had ever experienced. As a result of the intense bombing, a fearsome firestorm resulted and most of our relatives died. As usual we went to the basement and after a while, the air became hard to breathe and we went out into the street and saw fires all around us. The city had been bombed relentlessly for hours, which created the firestorm, as had been planned. We ran as fast as we could toward the river. But as we ran some phosphorus from a bomb hit my sister in the face and my stepfather scraped it off as fast as he could along with some of her skin which also came off. It was a most painful thing for her to experience. However, we did not stop; we kept running to the river where many others had already sought refuge. In all that hurry to escape, we forgot about the clothes and when we returned after the fires had died down (after many days), there was nothing left but the tub; all the clothes had been destroyed.

We had to go to a temporary shelter, because the house where our apartment was, had burned and was totally destroyed, as well as every other house in the neighborhood. The fire was so intense it was seen all the way to Frankfurt. It had been the heaviest bomber attack on the city and many thousands of people died, along with most of our relatives.

After the fires died down and the streets were cleared, the day came when we could actually go back and look for our relatives. When we came close to where we lived, a truck went by with a load of the victims and we saw a little girl fall off the truck bed and into the street. My stepfather came over to help and he recognized his little niece as the child that had fallen off the truck. It was a most gruesome experience, but we had to try to identify the relatives if we could find them in the rows of dead people on the street. After several hours my stepfather told me and my sister to go back to the shelter and wait for them there. Later we were evacuated to a farm on the outskirts of town and there we only heard the sound of the bombs as they fell on the city. None ever came close to us again.

Food was scarce at that time and we (as everyone else) had to resort to getting it any way we could. The farm had some milk cows and the farmer sold the milk, but never to us, as we were poor refugees who did not have enough money. I knew the young girl who milked the cows and she told me to put a container on a rope and let it out of the window and when she finished milking she would put some milk in it and we could pull it up, and so we had milk as long as we lived there. Times were extremely difficult for us and, indeed, all others living in the cities and even the countryside. Mostly everyone concentrated on survival for themselves and for any remaining family that they had. It was extremely difficult to find sufficient food to remain alive. The biggest sorrow was to see children without food and to be unable to alleviate the situation because we did not even have food for ourselves.

Peace at Last

When the war was finally over, we moved to Elfbuchenstrasse and we lived there until I left for America. My stepfather had secured a job with the Americans immediately after the war ended. This provided relief for our family. Additionally, I was able to find a job after the war and we tried to have a normal life again. All food was still rationed in Germany and other needed items were not available because of the general destruction of the country. It seemed that only the Americans had everything in abundance. Because of this material wealth the Americans had for themselves, many people tried to get jobs working for the U. S. Army. My stepfather worked as a truck driver and my sister and mother worked at the American hospital. So, all of us were employed and able to get ration cards. Without jobs, these cards were difficult to secure if you were an able bodied individual.

There were some college students in our neighborhood who knew how to speak English and my mother hired them to tutor all of us in English so that we could speak better and be understood by the Americans and also so we could understand them. Food and clothes and other household necessities were extremely difficult to obtain except on the black market. Here things could be obtained only if one had something to trade.

One day a girl I worked with asked me if I could dance and my answer was "Yes, of course I could". She then asked me if I could teach her and her American boy friend how to dance. He had a friend he would bring along and we could go to a place where there was a band and we could all learn how to dance. And that friend turned out to be Paul, the man I would later marry. Paul and his friend were stationed at Fritzlar, a small town not far from Kassel. That little town was still intact and therefore more suitable for the Americans. Kassel's few good buildings were mostly taken over by the Americans for office use and also living quarters for themselves.

Gradually our lives began to improve. Paul came over as often as he could and he and my stepfather played cards. We also all played board games together. Paul also brought us many things we were unable to obtain elsewhere. Mother and stepfather enjoyed the coffee and the cigarettes, which were trading items used to get other things on the black market. (At that time, American cigarettes were the accepted currency for black market trading.)

Our son Bernd was born in 1947 and because our papers for permission to marry did not arrive in time, we had to wait until later to get married. Then in 1949, Bernd and I left to go to America from Bremerhafen. Paul had to stay behind because his tour of duty was not complete. The ocean crossing was a terrible experience for me because I was seasick the entire time. There were some kindly stewards on the ship who looked after Bernd sometimes, when I was unable to do so. I was happy when we arrived in New York. There, someone helped me get on a train to Chattanooga, Tennessee, and an even bigger adventure was ahead.

Dysfunctional Aunt Kate

Paul's mother had died when he was a young boy and he was raised by his Aunt Kate, who came to the train station with her husband to meet us. When we arrived at the house where we were to live with them, I could not believe my eyes. The house was not finished. It had no siding, only black paper on the outside. Inside the wooden studs were visible and the toilet was an outhouse. At first, she was somewhat nice to us but I found out later that she was not happy at all that Paul and I were married.

I noticed something about her that to me was shocking and also repugnant. When she spit, it was black and some would remain on her lips. I wondered about this since my saliva was always white or clear and besides I considered it bad manners to go around spitting. My husband told me later that she dipped snuff. She also had a shotgun and told me that if I acted up in any way she would shoot me. As soon as my husband arrived home after his discharge from the army, she let us know that we better get married again at the local courthouse because that marriage in Germany was surely not legal.

Paul began looking for a job and soon found one. For the time being we had to live there with his aunt and her husband. She was so unspeakably rude and mean spirited that I wanted to leave and go back to Germany on the next boat available, even if Germany was in ruins and life in Germany was difficult. Regrettably, I had no money of my own for this.

I was too ashamed to write and tell my parents about my unhappy situation and so it was with a heavy heart that I stayed. This woman would beat my little boy unmercifully with a switch for the smallest transgression. She also told my husband and me that we could not sleep together in her house and that we had to sleep in separate rooms. I was so unhappy that I spent much time in tears.

That summer was so very hot. I remember washing dishes in the kitchen while she sat in the living room and watched TV with my husband. Then there was the occasion when I got my arm stuck in the wringer washer and Kate took an inordinate amount of time about getting me released. My arm turned blue and I was wracked with agonizing pain. Paul's brother and wife lived nearby and he and his wife were of a different mindset than the hateful Aunt Kate. They were very nice and considerate to Bernd and to me.

The days became so unbearable for me that one time, after the dysfunctional aunt beat my son again that I was determined to go to the nearby river and walk into it with my little boy and drown ourselves. But as we walked down the dirt road, I saw my husband's car come down the road and we hid in the bushes until he had passed. Then we came out again and walked again on the way to the river. When my husband came back and saw us, he wanted to know what we were doing there and I told him what happened and what I was resolved to do. From that day forward we no longer lived with the hateful Kate, but stayed with his brother for a few days until we found a small apartment where we lived until we bought a small house.

In the meantime, my sister in Germany decided that she would immigrate to Canada. Since she was alone it would be easy for her. When she got there and could work to save enough money, she would come to Chattanooga to visit with me. But it happened to be much different from what she had planned. She arrived in Canada, found a job and there met the man she would marry and she decided to stay in Canada. After working for a reasonable time, she was able to afford an apartment. That was when our mother and stepfather in Germany decided to come to Canada. They sold their possessions and came to live with Eva. Sometime later my stepfather came to visit us in Chattanooga and marveled at the beautiful mountains surrounding the city and said how much it reminded him of Kassel.

Parents Move to Chattanooga

Paul and my beloved stepfather got along very well together, so plans were made to move our mother and stepfather to Chattanooga as soon as possible. They bought a trailer, which we parked and had utilities hooked up in our own yard. My dad added a porch to the trailer and also made some improvements to our house. Dad also found a job and I was very happy to have my parents close by. We also had another addition to the family, our daughter Teresa was born and our little family was complete.

I was attending classes to get my American citizenship which I successfully completed and was later granted citizenship. Our son Bernd was drafted after he finished college, and soon thereafter he was sent to Viet Nam. Before being drafted, he had worked as a draftsman. After he returned from Viet Nam, he spent two weeks at home with us which were a most wonderful time for all of us.

Afterwards, Bernd went to South Carolina where he had earlier met a young lady who later became his wife. Her name was Glenda and she has been a wonderful daughter-in–law. They bought a small house next door and lived there until they found (and could afford) a larger one. Their first baby died shortly after birth; a very sad time for all of us. They later had a boy and a girl.

Bernd had his own successful business working as a draftsman. He and Glenda bought a larger house; however, soon tragedy struck again. Inexplicably, Bernd committed suicide. The reason is still unknown today to us, and all I know is that my world fell apart that day. I still mourn for him now as I know that I always will. Life must go on and several years later my adored stepfather became ill with cancer and died and mother went back to Canada to live with my sister Eva.

My husband had a really good friend, and he and his wife came over frequently to visit and we always enjoyed their company. The wife worked at K-Mart at the time and she was able to get me a job there in the pet department, a job I really liked. Those fish tanks have never been cleaner than when I cleaned them. Then after some years my husband became ill and when I asked for time off, I was told that if I took off that long I could not work there anymore. So I quit and stayed home and took care of my husband, Paul, who died soon thereafter from cancer.

After some time in the house alone, our daughter was married and I decided to move to an apartment. A friend of my son was building a duplex and I paid for a unit. I had good neighbors and many friends in Chattanooga and I frequently went to the cemetery to take care of the graves there and put flowers on them. My husband had bought gravesites for all of our family there.

One day my sister was visiting from Canada and she said she would like to visit my daughter who lived here in Madison. And while I was here the two of them persuaded me into moving here into an apartment that was reasonably priced and also I would be close to my daughter and her children. And so it happened that I left my beloved Chattanooga and now live in Madison, AL. Regrettably, I am unable go to take care of the graves of my beloved family in Chattanooga. I am now 84 and can honestly say that I never wanted to be this old.

Epilogue

Considering the situation of Anneliese and her sister Eva with the step mother, Tolstoy once opined that happy families are all happy in the same way, but unhappy families are unhappy in their own special ways. Happy families are composed of individuals that are not fixated on self, but value other members above self. They usually have and maintain a large number of friendships and once they are secure in food and shelter, they usually can be found doing community service, i.e. volunteer work at libraries, hospitals, church work, and other functions to give back service to the community. Clearly the step father and mother fit this sage observation, in that they were themselves happy individuals and were aware of the children's needs and provided for these children as best they could when they were in their custody.

Unhappy families are usually composed of individuals that are fixated on self, are more insular and have only a small group of friends if at all. Once they are secure in food and shelter, they usually do not provide volunteer community service, but many times are consumed with petty squabbles with other family members. From these sagacious observations, one could conclude that the stepmother and the Aunt Kate were most unhappy individuals and inflicted their pain on others whenever they could, probably without fully realizing the damage they were doing. In today's culture, they would be labeled "toxic relatives".

In the final analysis, once we are free from oppression, and reasonably financially secure, happiness is the responsibility of each individual. We can never expect or depend upon others to make us happy.

Anneliese now lives in the Madison, AL area and regularly attends social gatherings with the other ladies of Limestone County that share her experiences of being born in Germany before the war and finally emigrating to the U.S. However, since moving here from Chattanooga, she has lost all documentation from her past. She no longer has identification papers from Germany, or naturalization citizenship papers from the U.S.

Chapter 4
HILDEGARD

I was born in 1937 in Gross Chmeleschen, a small village of about 600 people, in Czechoslovakia (a nation created after WWI). I had 6 brothers and sisters. My parents had also been born there but were of Austrian citizenship. Later, after Hitler annexed the Sudetenland, we became Volksdeutsch or ethnic Germans.

My father's older brothers and sisters had careers or businesses, mostly in Berlin, Teplitz, and Vienna. Uncle Joseph lived in Prague and worked at the University of Prague, which dated from the 1300s and was the first German speaking university in Europe. My father joined him there as a student, but after two years he was called back by my grandfather to run the family farm.

We were descended from generations of farmers. My family was the tenth generation to farm the land and to live there. We had one of the larger farms, because they were one of the early five families that settled there

The house where I was born was built in the 1600s after our original village had been burned by protestant militants from the north during the 30 Years War. One of the earliest memories I have from home is my father carrying me on his shoulders to the main road in the village so I would have a better view of events. I remember one particular event were there were many soldiers on horseback riding into town. The entire village had turned out to view this procession and the people were jubilant! I later understood that this was 1939 and the Sudetenland had been annexed to Germany through the Münchner Abkommen treaty. This annexation did not bring many changes in our lives, other than German was again our official language, and all transactions could be performed in our mother tongue. We also used deutschmarks and school was again taught in German.

My father was an avid but discriminating hunter. He would go several times each year to observe the wildlife in our forest, especially deer. He would only shoot the less perfect so that the stronger could live and multiply. He did not hunt for sport, but only for food. My mother did not like hunting; she could not stand the sight of blood, much less the thought of shooting some living creature. During the war, even though we had a farm, we were only allowed to slaughter a limited number of various farm animals; but hunting was not restricted. On many of my father's observation trips, he would let me come along, even though I was only five or six years old. Hunting season was in winter, and the time to view the deer was late evening or at night. He would usually choose a special bright night when the moon was full. He would come to my bed and awaken me in the middle of the night and ask if I wanted to come along. I always said yes because this was a time and an activity with my father that I cherished.

My father and I would bundle up, as our winters were very severe, and then tiptoe out of the house. He would teach me how to check wind direction and would show me the open meadows in the woods, where the deer would most likely be. Sometimes we would have to go quite a distance out of the way, to make sure the wind did not carry our scent toward the area where the deer congregated. We also had to be careful not to step on fallen branches or dry leaves hidden under the snow cover because any noise would alert the deer. We did that by sliding our feet on the snow rather than taking steps. If the dominant stag got wind of us, he would schreck or bugle, and the entire herd would hightail it out of the meadow and into the thicket.

My father believed very strongly in only taking what we needed and then using all of it. He taught us respect for all living creatures, large and small. He believed we should live in harmony with nature as best we could and to always help other individuals who were in need. He knew what was good for us to eat, when to harvest it and what to leave in the forest. He loved nature, the natural order of things and taught me to appreciate this; a love which has lasted all my life.

My mother was a very good cook. She could make a feast from a rabbit that father brought home, or a pheasant, or some frog legs, or just a basket full of delicious mushrooms. Using various berries in summer, my mother would make Dalken, little pizzas, made with yeast dough and covered with fruit and Streussle. This was then baked and smothered with fresh whipped cream. Sometimes my mother would mash blueberries or wild strawberries, add sugar and cream, to make Wuchta, a flat roll, (almost like our English muffins). We would break the Wuchta, still warm, and add into fresh G'matsch; a fruit soup. This made a very refreshing supper on a hot summer night.

Mother could make raspberries into a heavenly syrup or juice. The syrup would be used all winter for toppings and diluted into drinks. Nuts, mostly hazelnuts and walnuts in the fall, were for eating fresh, or ground up for baking delicious Kipferln and Nusskuchen. We also grew poppies for making cakes and also for adding their seeds to various other dishes.

During the winter months when there was not much to do on the farm, my father would let me practice shooting a rifle. This was usually done by sticking a match on a fence post and hitting it at the right place; in the middle or one third down or on the bottom. This, of course, was preceded by safety lessons; the first one was "never point a rifle at a person or anything you would not consider shooting, whether the rifle is loaded or not". Being the sixth child, I thought that I was his favorite and only I had all those privileges. Only later did I realize that he did these things with all the other children. I also remember my mother letting me help carry lunch to the field for the workers who were hired during the harvest. In the fall, we harvested potatoes, which were first unearthed by a plow pulled by a couple of oxen (there was no fuel or mechanized farm equipment during the war). We piled all the dried potato tops at one end of the field and set them on fire. Into this we would throw some potatoes which we used to warm our hands, as it was usually very cold. Many times we would eat the potatoes to warm us from the inside out.

My father gave me the responsibility of caring for the first calf of the year. It was my duty to brush, feed and walk the calf around in the yard. Our other cattle were kept in stables instead of being allowed to roam openly. We also planted a Herzkirschenbaum or cherry tree in our orchard, and it was also my duty to water it during dry spells. This tree was given to my father by the University of Prague as part of a program to test new varieties of fruits for our area. The cherries were huge and delicious. I have only seen such big cherries one other time (in Italy at the south end of Lago Di Garda).

My father practiced vierfelderwirtschaft farming which means that he would rotate crops every year. Some areas were more suited for potatoes, because of the sandy soil, others for meadows, if close to a stream or lake. The grain crops, such as wheat, barley, oats, and legumes were rotated. Each farmer, in true conservation practice, left some fields bare and there he would spread natural fertilizer (well composted manure and vegetable scraps mixed with wood ashes), this was plowed under and the next year this field would be fertile for crops again. Because commercial fertilizer was not available, manure was also spread on the fields at the end of the year and plowed under. These would be the fields for next year's root crops. He also planted hedges between the fields for windbreaks, to help keep erosion at bay and at the same time provide shelter for different kinds of small animals and birds.

I wanted to do all the things my bigger brother was able to do. My two older sisters were 11 and 12 years older than I and not much fun for me to be around. Hedy, the oldest had left to attend a teachers college by the time I was six. Pauli, 11 yrs older, had other responsibilities around the house, such as helping my mother cook; which she loved and she also had additional farm chores. Rudy was 9 years older and away at school by the end of the war. He attended an agricultural college in Kaden. Karl was 7 yrs older and stayed at home to eventually take over the farm since he was a born farmer. Helmut was 4 yrs older and had to tolerate me, as he later complained.

I followed Helmut and his friends everywhere. He frequently allowed me to tag along. I remember hauling buckets of water from the creek to the woods where he had found fox boroughs. We each were stationed at one of the holes and on Helmut's command, poured water into the holes. At one hole, Helmut waited with a big stick to get the fox. I don't remember that we ever captured one.

Helmut always was the leader and his friends and I always did what he decided. There was one sad episode where he took ammunition caps from my father's supply. These were essential to ignite the powder behind bullets used by my father for hunting. Because it was war time, bullets and especially caps, were not readily available to hunters and my father carefully preserved his supplies. These caps were very strictly controlled and my father had to account to the government for them. Helmut and his friends took some and exploded them on the schoolhouse steps, by hitting them with a hammer.

When my father found out, he demanded an explanation and Helmut claimed that I had brought the caps to him and his friends. I was questioned and told the truth by denying it. Helmut's friends (at

Helmut's urging) one by one accused me; so my father ordered me to get the Schwartz Onkel which was a long black leather strap my father used to sharpen his razor. He counted the caps and found 32 missing. So I had to lean over his knee and got 32 + 3 licks for lying, on my bare bottom. It was my first spanking. I could not sit comfortably for several days. I did not speak to my father again for 2 1/2 years, until after being reunited with my family again after the end of the war.

School Days

I remember being told that I was old enough (about 5 yrs) to go with my aunt, Paula Schneider (my father's sister), and visit with her in her home in Woratschen. It was about 30km from our home by road, but closer by going across fields and down a steep hill where steps were hewn into the hill (Goldene Stiege über Bergwerk bei Kletscherdingen). We arrived at sunset, and after dinner I was bedded down on the couch in the living room. I remember that I kept coughing and sniffling, which I am sure was to get attention, because I was by myself in the strange room. I was not accustomed to being alone because there were 4 children at home and we all shared one bedroom. Aunt Paula came and gave me a little schnapps on a sugar cube to make my cough better. Before long I would beg: "Aunt Pauli a little more snapps, please". I could not pronounce schnapps. I had to listen to this phrase for a long time, as it was repeated many times, at various family gatherings, and always got a laugh.

The next morning, Aunt Paula took me across the street to the kindergarten with promises that I would have a great time with all the children there. I was assigned a play station, which was a desk with holes of different sizes and shapes in it and different pegs and a little hammer. I was to place the pegs into the right holes, square, triangular or round etc. (similar to the little Playschool benches). That did not please me, because I had been accustomed to doing real things all my life! So, when we were out in the yard during recess, I just went away into the nearby woods to escape. The teacher was a friend of my aunt, and my aunt checked with her that evening to determine the reason that I didn't come home after school. No one knew. Panic set in, and the whole village was mobilized to search for me. (It was wartime and we had Russian prisoners of war housed in barracks in the woods who worked cutting down trees etc.). I could observe the search action and after some time let my aunt know that if she promised I would never have to go to kindergarten again, I would come out of hiding. The next day my visit was ended and I was returned home.

In the fall of 1943, I started first grade, even though my birthday was beyond the official deadline of 31st of August. School was a one room schoolhouse. I was in the first row and my brother Karl, who was in 8th grade, was in the last row. Our teacher, Miss Schiffl, was young and very beautiful. One day, as she was inspecting our work, and leaning over to look at the papers, Karl lightly pinched her in the rear (he was 14). She was offended and told my father, but he made light of it telling her she was just too pretty. After a short time we had Miss Schindler, a different teacher, from the Reich which was Germany proper. We were considered Volksdeutsch, (ethnic German). She was very strict and not very well liked. She would make us stand at the beginning of class and raise our hand and say "Heil Hitler". In our village, the customary greeting was "Grüss Gott" (Greet God) and upon departing "Behüt' Dich Gott" or " Geh mit Gott", which roughly translates "the Lord's greetings" and "God with you". Our village was almost all Catholic and Miss Schindler was Protestant, which made her a curiosity to the children.

Helmut and my other sisters and brother Rudi, went to Bürgerschule in Jechnitz after the 5th grade where foreign languages and higher mathematics were taught. Karl was to take over the farm and my father thought it best not to send him there, as he might not want to stay on the farm. My father had gone to the University of Prague for two years and he was the youngest son of nine children. The oldest was, by custom, usually the one to take over the family farm. When his father called him home from the university to take over and run the farm, he at first was very unhappy about being on the farm and not at the university. His oldest brother, Anton, who traditionally would have gotten the farm, married a girl whose parents owned a restaurant in the next village. There she helped with the daily restaurant operation, including waiting on tables. That was not acceptable to my grandfather, who thought she would not make a good farmer's wife. Landowners or Bauern with a long line of proven ancestors, had their own standards called Bauernadel, of which my grandfather considered himself a member. I remember from early on having farm chores and responsibilities, which I relished. Until that time, land was the best security, especially after the post WWI depression.

Shortly after I started school, we began having an influx of refugees from the eastern parts of Europe. Mostly they were Ukrainians and a little later there were people from Silesia. We already had some individuals from German cities that had been bombed. The number of refugees was more than the population of our village. Everyone was required to take in refugees. These refugees were assigned quarters in private homes by the local authorities.

My father, as Ortsgruppenleiter (mayor), was in charge and he always took individual situations into consideration. We sheltered more refugees than required, because he always wanted to set a good example. My mother cooked for them as well as for us. We had no additional room in the house, because we still had five children (my youngest sister was born in 1944) and only three bedrooms. We needed all the rooms ourselves, because my grandfather also lived with us.

Later, hundreds of refugees from farther east (Ukraine, Hungary, Schlesien and the Balkan states) were also seeking shelter in our village. The school was converted into a Lager (camp), with bunk beds side by side, and every house and farm including ours, had more refugees than the owners had family members.

We still had a town crier, who would announce in the morning where and if we were to meet for class. Sometimes we met under the oak tree in the park, or in a meadow on the outskirts of town. Sometimes we just went on a field trip to collect blackberry leaves or Chamomile, Lindenblühten or rosehip for drying to make tea. This was sent to the cities or to the war front. The town crier also called out in case of emergencies, i.e. fire or after a snow storm, when all able bodied people in the village were required to manually clear the road halfway in each direction toward the next village so that buses could travel and also to make mail delivery possible.

During this time in the war, our daily lives were routine. My father spent much time hunting to provide extra meat, because we were under obligation to deliver a certain amount of our livestock and other harvest to the government to feed cities and troops. Authorities had inventoried our farm and decided how much of what we produced we would be permitted to use for our family and how much we were to supply to the government. The few items that we did not grow ourselves, i.e. sugar, paper products etc. were rationed. We made some sugar out of sugar beets, by chopping them in a large machine and boiling them in huge kettles down to a syrup. They were then poured into large jars to crystallize and then crushed to make a type of brown sugar.

Later, we did not know that the war was almost certainly lost. We constantly heard Hitler proclaim on the radio that we were winning on all fronts. All citizens were forbidden to listen to foreign broadcasts, under penalty of death. I remember sometimes in the evening someone would come to the house and my father would receive a quick whispered message and he would immediately leave. Only after the war did we learn that he went to caution others who he thought might be listening to Fremdsender (foreign broadcasts) that the Gestapo was coming. The Gestapo had the ability, by using equipment in their trucks, to determine which broadcasts people were listening to in their homes.

My father by then was Ortsgruppenleit;, before the annexation he was the youngest mayor ever elected in our village. Since he was the only farmer with some university education, he was the natural choice to be the leader. He also supported the independence of the German people and German culture, (more correctly Austrian because they were also German speaking).

Just before the Munich Treaty, the Czechs had called men to arms and my father was again called to active duty. He had previously served two years in the Czech military because he was born in 1900 and was 18 at the time of the creation of Czechoslovakia. He was among the first group of Austrians to serve in the Czech Army. At that time he was assigned as a scribe because he had beautiful handwriting. This second time that he was called, he left home and never reported in at the train station in the next village; therefore he was listed as a Dessateur. After annexation, this made him a hero to the new regime and he was made village Ortsgruppenleiter. He later told us that he did not report because he did not want to fight against his own people, including two of his brothers who lived in Berlin.

My great grandfather on my father's side had Hopfen Gartens (hop gardens), but when my grandfather took over, he decided to relocate them as they had been in the same area for a long time, perhaps thirty years. Over such a lengthy period, the soil becomes depleted of needed nutrients. In those days, there was no artificial fertilizer. Before he could rebuild them (they were very expensive and labor intensive to erect), the regulations changed, and no new hop gardens could be created because the country needed food crops to feed the growing cities.

Our village celebrated Kirchenfest or Kirchweih on the 24th of August each year and almost all of the relatives of the families in our village would come home for the celebrations. This was always a big family reunion. My mother baked and cooked for a week in preparation. There were boards put up on saw-horse supports in the yard and they were loaded with all kinds of delicious food; mostly small individual cakes topped with fruit, whipped cream, sausages, and salads of every variety. We always had much excitement and family stories were told and retold. That was the way we kept in touch with cousins and aunts and uncles whom we did not see all year. Of course it was also a time for the city folks to obtain baked goods and meat items that, due to rationing, were not available to them.

One very cold winter, the snow was above the 8' stone wall that encircled our house, yard, and large fruit orchard. A young deer jumped into our courtyard. A wolf, which was extremely rare in our area, was chasing and attacking it. My father rescued the deer and we cared for and nurtured it through the winter. We called it Bambi and it became our pet. In spring, when my father wanted to release it back into the wild, it would not go; it always followed my father back home, no matter how far he took it. So my father took it to his Hochstand (shooting stand); a place up in a tree where he could observe the area he was hunting. He had to wait a long time before it trotted away. He had marked it with a button in its ear. I was very sad, but he explained that it was where it belonged.

The following fall one of my father's friends came home on furlough from the front. My father loaned him one of his guns and gave him permission to hunt in our forest. He did not know about the markings for Bambi, and came back triumphantly, stating that he had bagged a deer on his first day. It was our Bambi which was not afraid of humans and therefore did not run away. I remember being heartbroken and crying for a long time.

A Typical Christmas

Because I came from Bohemia, our customs and traditions were a little different from those in Germany, even though our language was German. Our whole region of Bohemia was Catholic. In my home the Christmas season, which is usually cold, dark and gloomy; began with Advent, a time for fasting and penitence as a way to prepare for the coming of Christ. To symbolize the hope and anticipation of the coming of our Savior, a clergyman started the tradition of the Advent wreath by adding a candle on each end of a cross kept on his table. He added some evergreens; the symbol of life, which he arranged in a circle as the symbol of eternity. He lit one candle each week preceding Christmas, thus the Advent wreath was born. At our house it was suspended by red ribbons from the ceiling above the table. An Advent wreath has now become a tradition in many countries. We also had an Advent calendar, which kept the children's focus and attention directed toward Christmas. Each day one door or window on the calendar was opened to reveal a little surprise.

Following the beginning of Advent, we celebrated St. Nickolaus, whose Feast Day is the sixth of December. In my village, St. Nickolaus was dressed as a bishop. With him came his helper, Knecht Ruprecht (Knight Ruprecht), carrying a sack filled with apples and nuts, and Grampus dressed rather shabbily and wearing chains around his waist, presumably to carry off misbehaving children. St. Nickolaus and helpers usually arrived with lots of noise and commotion, giving us ample time to find a safe place close to Grossvater (grandfather) or mother. After entering the house with elaborate greetings and stories about the long journey, which seemed to put us somewhat at ease, St. Nickolaus would engage each child individually in conversation and ask about our achievements and if we behaved and listened to our elders. We then were encouraged to show what we had learned by singing a song or reciting a poem. After proving that we had been good, St. Nickolaus would pass out some apples or nuts, and if we had been exceptionally good, possibly a book. If we were bad Grampus rattled his chains and tied us up, and dragged us out into the darkness. After our pleading and promising to be better, he would release us. This experience usually encouraged us to cooperate with parents and siblings alike, until long after the holidays had passed and the weather was better so that we were able to expend our excessive energy outside again.

From St.Nickolaus day on there was a lot of hustle and bustle because my mother and my older sisters would be baking. Many of the traditional cookies, such as Lebkuchen, Zimtsterne, Aniseplätzchen, and Weihnachtstollen, are better after storage in airtight containers for a few weeks, usually in pretty tins with Christmas motifs. Sometimes the Stollen were wrapped in cloth, which had been soaked in rum.

This also became a time of family togetherness. Our kitchen was rather large, as it also served as our dining room and in winter as a family room. It was there that all the Christmas season activities were taking place. Our farmhouse did not have central heat; therefore the kitchen was the warmest and most comfortable place in the home. It was there that my grandfather would tell us stories of his childhood and so it became a place for lessons in family history. He also showed us how to bastel, which means to be creative. We made whistles and little baskets from willow branches and we cut shapes into raw potatoes and poured melted wax or lead into them to make ornaments and other toys. Even the girls had their own carving knives. We also made lanterns out of balsa wood or heavy construction paper. We cut Christmas motifs, such as Christmas trees, candles, stars, bells or angels, into the side panels and glued colored paper inside the cutouts so that when we lit the candle inside, it would give a stained glass effect. We took these to Mass on Christmas Eve to light our way because there were no streetlights in our village, and we walked in the snow. People from farther away came by buggy or horse-drawn sled. My grandfather and my father both played the violin, and both were in the church choir, and my aunt sang in the choir, too. They sometimes practiced at home, adding to the festive feeling. I do not remember my grandmother because she died when I was two years old.

During this time of the year the geese were being fattened by force feeding them a special diet of Gaensenockerln which is prepared from grains, eggs and boiled potatoes. This was to ensure a delicious Weihnachtsgänsebraten, or roasted goose, which was our traditional Christmas Day dinner. The geese chests were plucked of the fine down feathers which were saved to make the famous German feather beds that were an expected part of each daughter's dowry. Also the Karpfen (carp) were being readied for the Christmas Eve dinner. This was done by cleansing them of the muddy taste by catching them a few days ahead and letting them swim in a large tub of fresh water. Christmas Eve was still a Fast Day.

Christmas proper started with Heiligabend which means Blessed Evening or Holy Evening. While the children were kept busy with some of the above-mentioned activities, the freshly cut Weihnachtsbaum or Kristbaum (Christ's Tree), was being decorated in the living room, so the living room was off-limits to the younger children. The tree was decorated with real candles, lots of silver and gold colored glass ornaments, Lametta (or icicles and tinsel), candy, nuts, and fruit. When the candles were lit it became a sight of radiance and beauty.

Dinner on Christmas Eve always consisted of breaded fried carp, potato salad, and a salad of German lettuce (called Boston lettuce in the U.S.). After dinner we got ready for Metternacht or Midnight Mass. It was always very special because children on an ordinary day were not allowed to stay up this late. Also, the walk to church, which in our case was not very long, was nevertheless very beautiful with the snow glistening and with the stars very bright because there were no city lights in the village to diminish their sparkle.

Mass on this Holy Night was mostly a celebration with glorious songs. The children gathered about the nativity scene, where they placed their lanterns around the crib. Many of these beautiful Christmas carols such as Stille Nacht, Heilige Nacht und O Tannenbaum, O Tannenbaum have become famous throughout the world. Every time I hear them some of that childhood wonder returns and fills me with warm memories.

After mass on the way home we would search the sky for a glimpse of Kristkindel or Christ child, as we were sure that it was near.

Occasionally someone would see a falling star and our imaginations would run wild trying to guess if it was the Kristkindel and whether it had already come to our house. After arriving home we would gather in the large kitchen for some hot cider or other warm drink, all the while listening for the bells to ring, a sure sign of Kristkindel's presence, at which time we would storm into the living room where a wondrous sight awaited us. Seeing that Kristkindel had stopped at our house was always more exciting to us than the gifts, which usually were handmade wooden toys, maybe a doll, and always some clothes. We children believed Kristkindel brought the tree and gifts. I received a beautiful doll from my uncle in Berlin on the last Christmas at home. It was in a pretty box/bed with ruffles all around. The doll would open its eyes, had a pacifier and had the most beautiful long eyelashes and real hair. She was almost two feet long, with a velvet dress and leather shoes. All the little girls in our village came to ask if they could hold her.

Since most of my relatives were farmers, and in winter not much work can be done in the fields, this became a time to visit back and forth, hence all the cookies and cakes came in handy. Also, with every visit we would get some small present. This visiting usually continued until Epiphany, at which time the tree would be taken down, signaling the end of the Twelve Days of Christmas.

War Comes to Us

We did not have bombing raids on our village. The occasional Tiefflieger (low flying airplane), that for no obvious reason other than perhaps to amuse the pilot, would shoot at a farmer in the field. One farmer hiding under his horse was killed when the horse was shot and fell on the farmer. We had no other damage from the war, since we were the next to the last village before the Czech area. Because we were only agricultural and had no industry, the Allies did not find us to be a worthwhile bombing target.

As the war closed in on us I also remember seeing flares at night over Pilsen. We knew the Americans were coming and we all hoped they would get there before the Russians. But as we later learned the Americans were ordered to retreat and let the Russians have Bohemia. I remember on the 8th of May (it was my brother Karl's 14th Birthday) the town crier proclaiming that Germany had surrendered and that everyone had to assemble in front of their house. Those who had guns must bring them out to the soldiers and give them up. At this time the Czech partisans were driving into town on trucks. They stopped across from our house and came running toward us. My father had gathered his hunting rifles (he had several) and we were all in the yard. As he was going to take them to the trucks the partisans came running toward us with guns drawn. Hedy, my oldest sister who had come home on furlough, cried: "Father hide". My father replied; "I have not done anything to them so why should I run?" Hedy begged again, as it was obvious that they planned to shoot him. Instantly my father was gone, as if the earth had swallowed him. None of us saw where he went.

The Czech partisans came and one by one interrogated us as to where our father had gone, but we could not say. They bound Karl to an electric utility pole in front of our house and tortured him by slapping him first in the face with fists, then kicking him in the stomach until he collapsed and then continued kicking him. They would not let my mother or older sisters come to his aid. Then they took us into the house, (everyone else in the village was ordered to stay outside, while they were searching the houses). They shot 7 times into our ceiling (that's how many we were, including my grandfather). I believe that they were expecting that my father would think that they had shot us. But we learned later that my father had escaped into the fields and could not hear the shots.

As they searched house by house they killed an elderly gentleman who was bed ridden, simply because he could not go outside while they searched. They also tied my father's cousin, Karl Urban, by his feet and face down to the back of a horse-drawn wagon. They dragged him through the village, but when he tried to support himself with his hands and arms they broke them and they continued until he was dead. They claimed that he must have been a Nazi because he was not at the front. The reason he was home was that his two sons were on the Russian front and he was permitted to remain to run the family farm. After the fighting ended in our area most German speaking citizens were subjected to unspeakable tyranny by the Czechs.

It was announced that all non-native people had to leave the village by first light of the next morning. During the night my father returned. We packed a few things in one of our wagon and took our wagon, with one of the refugee's sons who lived with us, through the control point at the edge of the village. During the night we had gone out behind our house through the fields into the woods, where we waited for our wagon. When the caravan of refugees came past us, we joined our wagon and a little farther on broke away to go through Gossawoda to say goodbye to my mother's father. There we hitched up my grandfather's horses and tried to catch up with the others, but we could not immediately find them. Eventually we made it with thousands of others to the American line south of Eger where the Böhmerwald and Bayrischerwald share a common border. On the way there we met one Russian soldier on horseback, who came and offered my father a cigarette. He then went part way with us to get us through a few road blocks that the Czechs had erected to determine who was leaving. He told my father that he was ein Weissrusse (a white Russian) and was not a communist. He was with the Swoboda troops and a reconnaissance officer and spoke fairly good German. We did not see any other Russians at that time.

To our disappointment the Americans had just closed the border and we were not allowed into the American zone. So we had to stop and make camp in a meadow. At that time the Russian soldiers had not arrived in this area, even though we knew they were coming. My father, being concerned about my older sisters (the Russians were known to rape women), decided during the night that he, Hedy, and Pauli would cross the line and then find a way for us to get through. He was going to come back to get us the next day. In the interim, with all these people and horses and oxen, the creek became polluted because there was no sanitation and we were all ordered to return to our previous areas.

Karl hitched up the horses and we returned to my mother's father's farm. On the way we encountered many Russian soldiers on horseback. They came in rows, four abreast. We were in a very mountainous area on a narrow country road and on our side of the road was a very steep canyon. We looked down and saw many wagons, horses, people and also a baby in its buggy and they were all dead. They were callously and cruelly pushed over the side to make room for the advancing Russian soldiers. We were very afraid and hoped we would not be at a curve with the wagon at the same time the soldiers would be there. Mostly, the officers and NCOs were on horseback. The common soldiers were riding in wagons and were dirty and very shabby. We did not see any tanks or mechanized vehicles in that area or anywhere else near our villages. I think these vehicles were reserved for use in the big German cities.

At one point a Russian soldier stopped us and ordered Karl to give him one of my grandfather's horses (a Clydesdale, accustomed to pulling heavy wagons of hops to Pilsen and to bring back barrels of beer). He left us his riding horse, which had an infected wound on his spine where a part of a grenade was imbedded. In its current condition, the horse was not much help for pulling the wagon, but we had no choice. We knew that had we refused we would all have been instantly shot. When we arrived at my grandfather's house, the Russians were already there. My Aunt Franziska (Fanny) with her husband Julius Klimpel (an architect) were also there. Julius knew a little about medicine and he cleaned the wound on the riding horse and treated it with a homemade salve. Thankfully the horse did eventually heal. Because I grew up on a farm and loved animals it was painful for me to see that magnificent animal in such pain.

Every night the Russian soldiers came and searched for women. At dusk the ladies would all go into hiding. They hid in barns, under the hay, under stairwells, in attics, in the fields - anywhere they could find. There was a young girl Rita, about 17, who was living with my grandparents. She was at the farm to help my grandmother who had Parkinson's disease. Rita was a distant relative from the city and was there because all city youth had to put in time at a farm, (Landdienst). Also all farm youth were required to work in the city for a time. Rita came to my grandfather's farm and had no opportunity to get back to her parents at the end of the war. One night as she was sleeping between my grandparents (to slip under the cover between them if soldiers came), the Russians came, pulled back the covers and dragged her outside. I heard her scream but did not know what they were doing. Later she had to be taken to a hospital in the city of Jechnitz. I learned much later, when I knew what it meant, that she was brutally raped by seven soldiers. She lost her mind (she had been a virgin) and had to be placed in a mental institution. I had always thought she was one of the most beautiful girls I had ever seen, with raven black hair and pretty blue eyes.

My grandfather's neighbor in the village declared himself a Commissar because he claimed that he opposed Hitler and he thought this would save him and his wife from harm. However, he didn't trust the Russians and every night hid his wife in the village's electric transformer behind his house. He was the only one with a key. The Russian soldiers observed the people during the day and knew exactly where desirable women lived. One night they came and demanded he show his wife. He claimed that he did not know where she was. They shot and killed him instantly. No one in the village knew where his wife was hiding and days went by before someone heard her whimpers. She was almost half dead from dehydration and hunger before she was found and released from the transformer housing.

Occupation

The Russian occupation brought many ugly things with it, of which rape and murder were maybe the worst. The Russian officers and NCOs occupied the houses and usually very soon found themselves a Fräulein. Because most of these unfortunate women preferred to sleep with only one Russian instead of being frequently gang raped by an undisciplined dirty mob of thuggish soldiers, this became a unsettling though understandable arrangement. These sad women lived with the soldiers and were thereby protected from the nightly raids.

The enlisted soldiers were camped in the woods and descended upon the villages during the night to rape, plunder, and steal. Clearly the Officers and NCOs did not care what these uncivilized brutish soldiers did to the citizens, both men and women. There was no prohibition or retribution for gang raping women or for shooting and killing men who objected. Seemingly, the lawless Russian soldiers were totally without conscious or moral values that might have been an inhibition. It was almost as if they had reverted to some base animal instinct regarding sex, power and the instant fulfillment of their desires. It was a lawless and dangerous time.

Sometimes the soldiers would steal a pig or goose or anything else they could to cook and roast over fire pits. In retrospect, it seems clear that their army rations were woefully inadequate, along with their lack of manners and civility. During that dreadful time, I remember that my cousin Inge came every night to sleep with me because she was an only child and was two years younger than I. Her father was missing and later we found out that he was killed on the Russian front. Her mother hid each night and didn't want to leave Inge alone.

The Russians wanted to rape my mother on several occasions, but she would always carry my youngest sister Ingrid. She even slept with Ingrid on her chest and stomach. They sometimes put a gun to her head threatening to shoot her, but she would not let go of Ingrid. Incredibly, they never tried to take Ingrid from her.

All of this turmoil caused me to have nightmares. I was always dreaming the Russians were trying to kill me. I would try to run but in my dream I could never get away from them. One night I dreamed that I was killed. In my dream I could see my mother and relatives at the graveside crying. I was observing it all from above. I tried to tap on my mother's shoulder to let her know that I was alright, just different, I was still there but could not be seen. Somehow after that dream I never again was afraid of death because I knew that our spirit does not die. From then on in my dreams I would just fly away. During these times I would see the most beautiful landscapes, lakes, mountains, meadows with wildflowers etc. Many times when traveling, I would tell my husband that I feel as if I have been here and seen that before.

At home in Gross Chmeleschen we had a beautiful church, in Gossawoda. Other villages just had a small chapel with no priest. I told other children there about our beautiful church and they all agreed that they wanted to see it. So I arranged to meet my friends early Sunday morning and go to Chmeleschen for Mass. On Sunday morning, it was raining heavily and I went from house to house to get our group together. One by one they decided not to go. I set out by myself and took a shortcut through the woods. There many Russian soldiers were camped, most still asleep and I marched right through their camp. When I arrived in Chmeleschen, I tried to go to my Aunt Hedwig, my mother's sister, but she wasn't there anymore. Some Czechs had appropriated her house. I then went to the Levis, good friends of our family, and found Aunt Hedwig there helping with the household. The Levis could keep their farm, as they were of Jewish ancestry. (During Hitler's time, they went to our Catholic church. No one in the village turned them in and they remained safe). My aunt took off my soaked clothing and gave me a dress that belonged to my cousin, Hilde (she was only three days older than I), and I went on to Mass. My aunt hung my clothing near the wood burning stove to dry. When I got back, I changed and returned to Gossawoda. My mother was very upset when she learned that I had gone by myself.

On a few other occasions my mother prepared a basket with food and I took it to my aunt Pauli. She was imprisoned in Jechnitz for belonging to a ladies group ("Frauenschaft") that knitted socks, gloves, and scarves that went to the soldiers on the front. Germans were not allowed to leave their villages without special permission and we were to wear white armbands. I had no permission to leave, so I pretended that I was Czech by singing a phrase of a song that I had heard the Russian soldiers sing when they got together at night to drink vodka. I am now sure that I did not deceive anyone, but I was a small child and did not know any better. In order for the Russian soldiers to drink vodka at night they had to brew it themselves. Pan Niek, the soldier who occupied my grandfather's house, set up a still in one of the sheds. He did not trust us thinking we might slip some poison into it. So when the vodka was ready he made us children, mostly Helmut and me, drink a glass full of the still warm brew. This made us very tipsy and ill; I remember falling into a ditch one time after being forced to drink a glass.

Mr. Liszner, who was a Czech citizen and well known to all of us, had lived in our village all through the Hitler time. Liszner and a few other Czech families had all lived in peace with the village people. The Czech children attended school in Cista, two villages away, which was mostly a Czech village. During the Hitler time he frequently came to my father to tell him he wanted to join the Party. My father always questioned why he would want to do that. Liszner was the only one in our village with a truck and was able to buy food items for his family from Cista. He could get oranges and other fruits which we could not get because of the embargoes. He needed papers (Grenzübertritt) to cross into the Czech area, and my father was the one to issue these, since he was also the Honorable Justice of the Peace. Mr. Liszner sometimes brought an orange, chocolate or other small treat for us, but my father always refused to let us accept it. He was very strict about rules and didn't want the appearance of exploiting his position to benefit himself or his family.

Now under the new regime Liszner became a high ranking Communist official and was in charge of our area. He found out that we were at my grandfather's house and ordered us to return home to run the farm. By now the Russians had arrived and the Czech partisans were gone, which made it safer for us. We had no choice but to return. Karl and Helmut now had the responsibility to take care of everything on the farm. We had brought our wagon with the few valuable possessions that we had originally taken with us, such as money, gold coins, my mother's jewelry, family pictures etc. We had with us all that was of either sentimental or monetary value.

We had been there only three or four weeks, when a Czech individual with a suitcase, umbrella and his son appeared. It was at dinner time and my mother had just set the table. He said, "Thank you Frauchen (beloved lady). This is ours now and we will eat this and you will have two hours to collect any items you wish to take with you and then you must leave. But if times should change and you are permitted to return, we will leave." My mother went through the house and collected a few of her valuable items. He then came and took these from her and thanked her again for finding everything for him. As most of the village people had done, we tried to hide our valuables. This time we were not allowed to carry anything with us, so what we were wearing was what we had. We again went to my mother's father's farm, except this time on foot.

Within a few months we were expelled from our grandfather's home and sent to refuge camps. The first was in Jechnitz, where we were housed in a hotel ballroom that had been converted to a camp. Each family had a spot where we could sleep; there were no walls separating people. We slept in our cloths on the floor. It was a holding camp until the authorities could collect a trainload of refugees. From there we were transported in cattle cars with no sanitary facilities other than a hole in one corner on the floor. We were old and young; all pressed together standing only, no place to sit down. If a pregnant lady should faint, she could not fall down. At night they stopped the train and all had to disembark to get some soup or other meager nourishment, from a big kettle over an open fire provided by Russian soldiers. This routine went on for several days. We all thought we were being transported to some camp in Siberia or other Russian destination. I think now that we were just taken in circles. There were no windows in the cattle cars and at night we would usually stop in a forest. If a death or birth occurred in the cattle car, those people would be taken off the train. We never knew what happened to a new born and its mother. Even though we were born in Bohemia (Sudetenland, now the Czech Republic) we were expelled because of our ethnicity. We had to live in refugee camps in the Russian sector under terrible conditions. A total of 15 million ethnic Germans were expelled from the Eastern countries after WWII.

While in refugee camps we had no school. There was no consideration for hygiene or even food that would nourish us. Eventually I was living with my uncle Karl, my father's brother. He had been bombed out of his house and his restaurant and his wholesale liquor store had been confiscated. He, my aunt and cousin lived in an apartment in East Berlin where I started second grade. Berlin was completely in ruins. To get to school we had to go over ruins of houses, some which had not completely collapsed. Women were everywhere cleaning bricks and sorting them. The Russians occupied the eastern part of Berlin and Russian soldiers were seen at times. Because we had nothing to trade for food, and money wasn't worth anything, we had very little to eat. Warm clothing was not available. I froze my small toes during one of the harshest winters because the only shoes I had were made of straw.

Several of my uncles did not return from the Russian front. Sadly, my step grandmother died of starvation in the refugee camp where she was imprisoned. She was not with us or with any other family members. My grandmother had Parkinson's disease and could not stand in line to receive the meager rations that were available, nor did she have any utensils with which to try to eat. I feel certain that I lost my parents (father at 56 and mother at 55) prematurely, because of the turmoil and hardship imposed on them by the horrid conditions we all experienced after the war.

My father and older sisters had been able to escape through the forest to the west and he was looking for work and a place to live, which was a requirement to bring the remainder of the family to West Germany. He found a job helping rebuild the bridge across the Rhine River in Maxau near Karlsruhe. By the time I arrived they already found a place to live in Knielingen, or West Karlsruhe. After two years my family was reunited; my father was finally able to get permission for me to join the family. To come to the west from Berlin I had to have the correct papers. These my father had gotten for me and were for the purpose of reuniting families. The Russians did not care about a 10 year old child; I was of no use to them. My cousin, who lived in the American zone, was allowed to travel and was with me. We had to ride a special train that could not stop on the way through East Germany. I was most anxious to see my family again.

There was one unforgettably horrible incident that occurred on the train. Another girl my age, who was also being reunited with her family in Kölln, and I were standing by a door. Most adults were dozing or sleeping because it was night. She leaned against the door and it swung open and she fell out. I first tried to hold her, but she was holding on to the door handle and the door flew open and the train was travelling at a fast speed. I screamed and yelled but I couldn't reach the emergency brake cord which was too high for me. It took several moments for the adults to understand the situation. The train was stopped and we backed up for quite some distance. The rescue team was carrying flashlights and all I could see was that she was carried away on a stretcher. I don't know if she was still alive or if we were already on the west or still on the east side of the border.

We had become instant friends, probably because of our past experiences were so similar and we were near the same age. We had also talked together for much of the time we had been on the train.

Mostly we were telling each other how happy and excited we were to finally see our families. We also spoke about exchanging addresses so that we would stay in touch, but we had to wait for the adults to wake to get some paper to write down our information. I can vividly remember the details of that tragic night, but sadly, I no longer remember the name of this unfortunate young girl.

I had a difficult time after arriving in the west. I had a very strong Berliner accent. In Knielingen, people spoke a Badenzer dialect. I could not understand them and they did not like my way of speaking, so many times after school I was beaten up. Once I placed a stick beside a front garden fence, and after rounding the corner I took the stick and beat the boys who were always beating on me. After that I never again was bothered by anyone.

My brother Rudi was not with us when we left our home. He had been away at an agricultural university in Kaden. Just before the end of the war he and his fellow students were required by the German government to serve on the Russian front. We did not know that he had been dressed in a dead SS officer's uniform because the German clothing industry had been destroyed. He was captured by the Russians and severely beaten. When the Russians realized that they were just young students and did not have the SS tattoo mark under their arms, they treated them a little better. At least there was no immediate threat of execution. He and his friends were then sent to Prague, because they said they were from Bohemia. They had to march from Prague to Tabor. On the way the Czechs partisans beat and killed many of the captured students.

Eventually we all made it to West Germany, where I grew up in Karlsruhe after a two year separation from my family. By the time I was reunited with my family, things had improved a little and we lived in an old abandoned schoolhouse. Each classroom was divided into two family units. We, three of my brothers, my younger sister and I and my parents, lived on one side, on the other side was the

Blum family from East Prussia, with parents, three children, and a grandmother. There were a total of four class rooms divided up for eight families. The lower level of the school was used as a Turnhalle or gym. There was one sink in the hallway; the toilets were downstairs and there was no water or lavatories for washing.

Eventually we were able to move to a new house with three bedrooms. My father bought beautiful antique furniture very reasonably from an estate sale, because it seemed that the young people wanted modern Danish furniture. He also secured a job as a curator in the museum. At this time his health was poor and construction work was not a good choice for someone with heart problems. Unfortunately he also had been hit by a truck while riding his bicycle home from work. It caused a blood clod and he also suffered from a broken arm.

By 1948 we had the Währung and the country was issued new money. At last we could buy food and other needed items again. Thankfully the Marshall Plan changed the allied relationships with Germany. Before that the German people were still seen as enemies and treated as such.

The numerous deportees and refugee children had been added to the local community. This was more than the school's capacity, which had been built for the local student body. Our homework was tremendous. We had very few books, since the books from the Reich were not allowed and the new ones that were being written with Allied approval were not available. So during the school hours we mostly had to write notes and copy text, which we had to study at home. When I started fourth grade, a new concept was being tested and the best students from three classes were chosen to start in the Sprachklasse or Sonderklasse. We began studying English and in the fifth grade French was added. Our teacher, Fräulein Jerger, was our teacher all the way through eighth grade. I skipped eighth grade and entered the Karlsruher Höhere Handelschule, where we mostly studied business subjects such as shorthand, bookkeeping, typewriting, English, French, mathematics, and general business practices.

After graduating from grade school I attended Karlsruher Höhere Handelschule which was similar to an American business college. After graduating from there I started working for Kaloderma, at that time one of the oldest and biggest cosmetic companies in Germany. There I worked in various capacities, first in archives, then in coordinating and scheduling the salesmen who traveled all over West Germany. My final job with this firm was market research.

It was a very good company with generous salaries and many amenities, such as tennis courts, a Kantine with very affordable three course meals at noon, childcare, a greenhouse etc. all of which we could use. Also, we could spend our vacation time using the facilities of the company. We could go (free) for up to four weeks to one of the company spas. One spa was in the Black Forest and one near the North Sea. Vacation time was very generous, starting with two weeks the first year and increasing by an extra week after the next two years until four weeks were allotted. Hedy and Pauli had found jobs in a different town. Hedy was a translator and Pauli worked in an American mess hall to get food.

My father was the kindest man I have ever known. He tried to help everyone. One day he brought a man to the house (we still were in the cramped schoolhouse). The man looked very bad, almost as if he was near death. He was dressed in very old ragged clothes which were dirty and soaked from rain. It was near supper time and my mother took my father aside and asked what he had in mind? My father said to let him get warm and to have something to eat. My mother said that we had hardly anything for ourselves. My father replied, "Everyone will just take one bite less and then he will also have something." The man had just been released from a Russian prison camp where he had become infected with tuberculosis and he had no place to go. He was also from Bohemia and did not know where his wife was or even if she was still alive. When my father found him he was sitting beside the street in the gutters. He later told us that he was planning to commit suicide but my father gave him hope. He later found his wife in the eastern sector and they were reunited. He became a successful salesman, and was a family friend for life. His wife was the one who later gave me a combination birthday /engagement party.

Epilogue

In retrospect, as an adult it is shocking to remember that grandmother died of starvation in a refugee camp because she had Parkinson's, couldn't stand in line for the meager provisions offered and also had no utensils to receive these meager provisions. German society was for many centuries, acclaimed for its high level of culture, refinement and achievement in the arts, music, literature and science. There have always been many individuals who are highly educated with a huge preponderance of citizens speaking multiple languages, even in the villages. Catholic and Protestant churches abounded and were well attended at that time in history. Surely Nazism could not have erased this culture and rich heritage in the short time that it prevailed. Sadly, one can only surmise that under extreme privation, a high preponderance of people will revert to the basest behavior of "every man for himself". The Russian soldiers' and the Czech partisans' unspeakable behavior towards the people of the villages clearly supports the premise that not everyone in our modern world is civilized.

Equally incomprehensible was the expulsion of families and other villagers from homes and the wanton seizure of properties, seemingly only because of Germanic heritage. There was no underground resistance movement in the village or among the people of other nearby villages. Equally mystifying is the wanton savagery that the authorities permitted the Czech partisans and the Russian soldiers to inflict upon the civilian population. Some of us survived, but many were tortured, murdered or executed without cause (Karl Urban). It was an irrational time and place without understanding. It was a fortunate escape to freedom.

There is a small book "NEMESIS OF POTTSDAM" authored by an American lawyer from New York, which documents in detail the accounts of the expulsion and atrocities that were inflicted on us. I had the privilege in 1977 to read his manuscript and give my opinion. I just confirmed his story with the caveat that each family or group had slightly different experiences. I was a child at the time, but now as an adult I can understand the horror that the adults must have experienced.

After the war my oldest sister was a translator for the German police and interacted with American constables. She met her husband through this activity and they were married in 1948 and moved to America. They were later stationed in Vicenza, Italy. My future husband was in the same battalion as my brother-in-law and was their friend. I went on vacation in May 1957 to see my sister. At that time, I had a German boyfriend that my parents liked very much. They were not pleased that I agreed to correspond with my future husband, even though there was no talk of marriage. My boyfriend strongly objected to my writing to an "Ami" (mildly derogatory term for an American). I have always been a very strong willed person. This objection was unacceptable and eventually we parted.

My future husband came through Karlsruhe on his way to visit his brother in Frankfort. He stopped by and I agreed to go with him to meet his brother. Of course, I brought my little sister and my aunt along. My parents had already died; first my father of heart failure and two weeks later my mother. I believe that she was unable to cope with the events suddenly engulfing her.

My husband made a career of the army and my only issue was that we moved too often. By the time my husband retired (he spent 30 years in the military), we had moved 25 times with Huntsville, AL, our last duty station. With four boys our moves were not always easy. But as a whole I enjoyed military life very much. As soon as I was eligible to get my U.S. citizenship I applied and became a citizen in 1963 in El Paso, Texas.

Since our retirement we have enjoyed volunteering in various state and national parks and state fisheries in Idaho, Oregon, Washington state and the Rocky Mountain National Park. I volunteer in summer at the Pikes Peak Historical Museum and my husband volunteers as a member of the sheriff''s posse in Teller County, CO. In Huntsville my husband serves as a tax assistant for military personnel. We both feel blessed and enjoy giving back to "our" country that we both love.

We keep in contact with my family in Germany. My brothers have come to visit us and so have some of my cousins, nieces and nephews. One of my nephew's daughters just spent six months with our son in El Paso before starting college. I have gone back several times to visit family and friends. To our disappointment my husband was never stationed in Germany.

I would be remiss if I did not mention how friendly and helpful most of my American neighbors were. Usually we lived in military communities or near them. Whenever we moved, no sooner did the moving van arrive, than the neighbors would be there with a pot of coffee or sometimes even a cake to welcome us. Sometimes the neighbors would offer to have our children come and play with their children. This was to keep the children from getting underfoot while the movers were there.

When I was growing up I always felt that the entire village was like a big family and most members were well loved. The war and the ensuing horrors made me realize that this was a halcyon time in my early childhood and is to be remembered.

Chapter 5
ANNEMARIE

I was born in 1932 in Eltville, on the banks of the Rhine River close to Rüdesheim, Germany. Our family consisted of my parents and four sisters, so altogether we were five girls. Our home was in the country where my parents operated a large nursery that grew vegetables for restaurants. There were hot springs where people came for the baths and mud packs that were said to be beneficial to your health. The Doctors would prescribe a week of spa as part of a treatment for someone who seemed to be in need of some physical recreation or emotional renewal.

Father was the head gardener and he had seven men working for him. He had contracts with the hotels where the restaurants were located to provide much of what they needed and so our days were spent outside working with our parents. We also grew strawberries and flowers which were sold on market day. It was hard work for all of us, but in retrospect it was a peaceful time and the whole family worked together. Our lives were very satisfactory because in addition to the immediate family, our grandparents and aunts and uncles lived nearby.

In 1939 father was drafted into the German Air Force and his assignment was to lookout for enemy planes which sometimes were not very far away. Usually, he was able to come home every week or so for a few days. I never really knew what else he did. Looking back now; he must have been in some kind of communication unit.

Later in the war, our lives changed because we had to do all the work ourselves. Most of the men were in the armed forces and there was a shortage of able bodied men to work. Food was scarce during the war, even though we had vegetables and fruit, we needed milk. Nearby was a dairy farm and when enemy planes flew over in the 1940s and if the dairy trucks happened to be outside, the bullets from the planes would puncture the big milk containers. Our mother sent us out with little containers to catch the milk that was squirting out. Also all the school children were sent to pick up leaflets dropped by planes, (written in German) telling the people to give up and surrender. We also picked up aluminum strips that were dropped by the planes. This was dangerous because we were outside not knowing when the next planes would fly overhead and start shooting again.

When sirens were sounded in nearby Wiesbaden, my mother, my sisters and I ran to a shelter we had built in the field. It was just a big hole in the ground with wood beams across the top and then straw on top of that. It really was no protection other than if planes came down to strafe the fields while we were working there, we could jump in there and be relatively safe because we were not visible. The biggest concern was that bombs would be dropped on us. When we saw and heard the many planes going across our area, we were petrified with fear. Of course, their goals were the larger cities where the factories that supported the war effort were, but as children we had no idea of all that. We had several relatives who died in Wiesbaden, which was heavily bombed and mostly destroyed. When we were in our house or close to it and the sirens sounded, we went into the basement to hide until the all clear signal was given. It was an old house, built in 1850, and was where we had always lived.

I remember those last days before the Americans came. We practically lived in the basement where we had made beds of straw. As the war was ending, there was a young German Lieutenant hiding in the horse barn and the Americans were still shooting it out with a remnant of German soldiers who were in our little town. The American artillery did a lot of damage to the houses in the town and several people lost their lives. We had a lady from Wiesbaden, who was an English teacher and came to live in our village when the bombings became too frequent. She told us not to be afraid when the Americans came because she would speak to them on our behalf. Sadly, she was so poor that she carried all her belongings in an old baby buggy. She was elderly, as I remember, and my family made a straw bed for her in our basement and she stayed there with us. Unfortunately she died several days before the Americans arrived.

Everyone was afraid to go outside because we were fearful of being shot. After spending all that time in the basement, to this day I am deathly afraid of closed in spaces or rooms without windows. Once when I had to get an MRI, they had to stop it after a few minutes because I became violently ill. I had a reaction to the closed in space and I really believed that my heart would stop.

When the Americans came closer, the mayor of the town and others got a white flag out and started walking up the hill in the direction where they knew the Americans where and there surrendered the town and surrounding areas. The Mayor was a dedicated member of the Nazi party, but he did not tell anyone. In the meantime, when the shooting stopped and everyone got out of their basements, my mother told my sisters and me to hide; she was afraid of what could happen next. We saw the Americans come closer, all with guns in their hands and then we heard them speak fluent German. They were Jewish Americans who had lived in Germany before the war and now were in special units because of their language skills.

Many of the German military men who were in the vicinity also came toward the town. I do not know if they were in uniform or not, but they were all captured by the Americans and became POWs. My father was among them and he was sent to southern France and did not return to us until 1948. We did not know where he was and when my mother heard that there were some German prisoners nearby; she sent some of us to go see if our father might be there. We went, but in vain, our father was not with those prisoners.

Then not long after, all the other Americans came and started looking for places to stay and to live temporarily. A curfew was imposed and we could leave the house only one hour in the morning and one hour at night. After that, many refugees came to our town and my mother took in as many as she possibly could. These people had lost everything they had in the bombed out cities around us and now were looking for a place to live and start life all over again. Our house was always full and many people gladly slept in the barn until better arrangements could be made.

Later, when more of the Americans came, they took over all the hotels. My mother sent my sisters and me out to ask the GI's if they needed their laundry done. And so it was that we went into the laundry business. Another older lady was hired later and our business was growing. There was just one thing that was not available to us and that was clothes dryer! In that very cold winter of 1945/46, the clothes froze on the outside line and then had to be thawed out again to be ironed and have ready for pick up in a day or so. We all worked very hard, since our life literally depended on the Americans and we needed to do a good job. I remember my mother staying up all night sometimes to get the laundry ready for the next day.

We were paid in cigarettes, peanut butter, soap and candy. Then my mother would send my sisters and me into the nearby countryside to trade those things to the farmers for bacon, flour and other things we did not have. We were told, in no uncertain terms, not to eat the chocolate and the other candy, only to use it to trade for things we needed. So we walked and walked all day, sometimes more than 20 miles and we were not always welcomed by the people on whose doors we knocked. Other obstacles were the tanks and soldiers who were stationed on the entrance and exits of each little village to keep the civilians from going out. We carefully and surreptitiously crossed the fields to get around them. There was never enough food, no matter how hard we tried to get the most for the things we had to trade. My mother gave us each our own loaf of bread and we had to make do with it until next week when new bread was available. Sometimes my older sister Margot gave me some of her bread since I ran out early. We were always hungry.

The German POWs who worked for the Americans in the mess hall in town told us children to wait in the ditch along the road in the evenings when they came by on the trucks to return to the camp where they were interned. They would throw American bread out to us. We were so happy to have that white bread, it tasted like cake. It was clear that the American drivers of those trucks and also the American armed guards knew what those POWs were doing, because they never stopped anyone from throwing things to us. My mother once made a cake with whatever she had and we carried it up to the camp to give to those men who were so good to us and threw the bread out. There we heard about the leftover food from the mess hall that was put in containers and anyone could come and get it. What a joy, we got leftover pancakes and all kinds of food we were not used to having, but it was good.

Our mother became very ill during that time and we did not think that she would live. There was no doctor and available nurses could only help with advice. Fortunately, mother finally got well. I have often wondered how she endured during that terribly hard time without any help, especially the responsibility to provide care for my four sisters and myself.

Early in 1948, when the Deutsch Mark was introduced, we again started selling vegetables and strawberries and mother was able to save some money. For us, things were slowly becoming better. The town was selling some land later that year and mother bought a piece of land just outside the town and not far from where we lived. She said that one day she wanted a new house and it would be built there, on her own land.

When my father came back home, he started to work in the nursery business again, supplying the hotel restaurants with vegetables and fruit. He was able to hire several men and business started to improve. He was able to pay these men to help him build a new house on the land that mother had bought. First it took a long time to dig the big hole for the foundation of the house and the future basement.

After things became better for us, I went to Wiesbaden to attend school for specialized training in the hotel business. I worked in the hotel and also attended school several days a week. We had to work six weeks in the kitchen, six weeks in the dining room, the bar and get familiar with all the work that was necessary to run a successful hotel.

My future husband was stationed in Wiesbaden at Camp Perry, and on the weekends the soldiers came to the hotel where I worked. They had a special table always reserved for them where they ate the good German food and drank the German beer they all liked. I did not speak any English at the time and one of the waiters told me that there was one soldier who said every week that he was going to marry me. Oh how crazy is that guy? I have a German boyfriend and I don't even understand that American. But somehow we managed to get acquainted.

He had a driver who was from Texas and the driver spoke some German. He would translate what we said and that is how we communicated. We would meet at a little park close to the bus stop where I caught the bus to go home. He always wanted to know where I lived but I would not tell him because I did not want my family to know that I had started dating an American. But some people who rode the same bus home as I did told my mother that they had seen me on the park bench kissing an American soldier.

When I came home a few days later (I stayed at the school some of the days), she stated that someone had told her they saw me in the park with an American. I denied it, of course, and went back to Wiesbaden the next day and then saw my American soldier in the park again. I liked him and he let me smoke, which was all the rage in those days, especially if you smoked American cigarettes. And so we kept on meeting and other people from my village saw me and again told my mother that they saw Annemarie on the park bench with an American.

The next time I came home my mother asked me again if I saw an American in Wiesbaden and again I lied. Then she said, don't lie to me, another person told me they saw you again with an American. By that time I was only twenty, so when I went back to Wiesbaden and saw my American, I told him that I could not see him anymore because my parents would punish me if I did. After he asked me again where I lived I told him the name of the town and that was all and I was sure that that was it for us. Little did I know what he was going to do? He found out where I lived and when I came home there was his jeep in front of my house. Oh no, what now? I was so afraid of what my parents would say and do!

I was terrified to go into the house but finally managed to do it. When I walked in Walter, the friend my husband had who spoke German, said to me that my parents wanted to speak with me. My heart was beating so fast it almost seemed to jump out of my chest. My mother pointed out to me that I realized that my reputation was gone since I had been seen with an American, but that Ray had offered to marry me and that I should decide what it was I wanted to do. Walter and Ray had spent the whole afternoon with my parents and again the next day while I was at work. So when I came home that evening they were all there eating and drinking apple wine and all was well. My father said that he had nothing against Ray, that the soldiers that took him prisoner after the war ended had a job to do. They were all in agreement that life was much better now and there was no animosity between them anymore. We started discussing the paperwork that we needed to get married and when he brought them to me, I was flabbergasted! How could I ever answer all the questions when I could not understand what they were and what they meant?

By then he was transferred to Augsburg. I did not know how to speak English, let alone write it. I never got a letter from Ray and anguished over what was happening. My mother was upset and said it was a terrible thing to lose one's reputation and then get left in shame when all the world knew I was engaged to an American. Who knows if he would return and why did he not write and let me know something? My heart sank and I could only hope Ray would come back. My mother said those kids he showed on the pictures were probably his and were just lies he told and who knows where is he now?

Two months went by and I finally got up enough courage to go to Camp Perry to find out where Ray was and how I could get in touch with him. Standing there in front of that gate, I thought of that popular war time song "Lily Marlene" who stood at the gate under the street light waiting for her soldier. I just wanted to talk to someone and ask him about Ray. I finally got in touch with Walter and I asked him about Ray, but he would not tell me anything other than that Ray was in Augsburg.

In the hotel where the soldiers ate, I would ask the other soldiers if anyone heard from Ray and they always said no. But one day when I went home again there was Ray and he told us the whole story. Since he had not heard from me, he got a weekend pass and came back to Wiesbaden to look me up and find out why! Then he said that he wrote and told Walter to deliver the letters and translate them for me, something Walter never did. The truth was that Walter wanted me for a girlfriend and just ignored the letters. And the pictures of the children he had shown me were his sisters children, all nine of them. So we were able to straighten all that out and my parents and I were very happy. So late evening rolled around and Ray asked me when the last bus went to Wiesbaden. But it was Saturday and the last bus had already gone and the next one was not until Sunday morning. Mother would let Ray stay all night, but not sleep anywhere and she stayed up and made coffee and waited for the earliest bus to leave. I got up early and we both went to the barracks where Walter was billeted.

I had to stay outside and wait. Soon I heard a big commotion and noise and then the MP's came running and went in to the barracks to see what was happening. Ray found out that Walter had kept all the letters and they got into a big fight because of that. Ray took all the letters and came out and showed them to me. We started again with our wedding plans. He had to go back to Augsburg and I had to fill out a plethora of papers before we were finally married. We had a small apartment there and I became pregnant right away.

Our next document war began with my applications to obtain a visa for America and a German passport. By then, several months passed and Ray was transferred back to the States and my papers were not ready! That was an anxious time for me, wondering how it all would work out and how was I going to be able to join my husband. The year was 1953 and I had to have help with everything that had to do with the English language since I still could only speak very little. After our baby girl was born, she got her passport right away and we got our orders to go join Ray. The plane ride was a very long one, I was sick and with a baby to attend, it was difficult to deal with real diapers and feeding. I was happy to finally arrive in New York.

Ray was there to meet us and we got on a bus for a long ride to Chicago where his brother met us up for the next journey to where the family lived in Iowa. They were all happy to finally see us and I was happy to have a few days of rest. But then reporters came from the local Newspaper and wanted to interview me.

Since I did not understand what they asked, Ray would speak for me after he told me the question. We had our own language between us and he understood what I said. He probably told them a lot of stuff that I never told him to say, but I did not care what was said, I was still ill. Taking care of my baby and myself was all I was concerned about. Soon Ray went to his next duty station at Fort Leonard Wood, Mo. In the meantime I was pregnant again and when we moved to Missouri, we lived in a one bedroom trailer and then a small cabin. The weather was so very hot. It was a heat the likes of which I had never experienced in Germany. We had plastic curtains on the window and I was absolutely miserable. I walked to a little store and bought watermelon, something new to me. I ate jello and cherry pie and all the good things that I never had before and promptly got very sick. I was eating all the things I should not have been eating, but did anyway because they tasted so very good to me. The doctor had warned me not to eat all that, but to eat only good things, since things like that made me feel bad, in my condition. Our son was born in the old barracks hospital on the post.

Ray had an aunt who lived nearby in Lebanon, Mo and she took care of our little girl while I was in the hospital. When Ray took me to the hospital he checked me in, the nurse told him to take my clothes with him and they would call when the baby was born. I was deathly afraid to be there and things went from bad to worse. I had a spinal to numb the pain and I did not understand what they were doing and then when the baby was born I was put in a room by myself, because they did not know if the baby would live. I tried to get out of bed with my legs still numb and that did not work out well. It was a nightmare and I have never been a good patient since then. They called Ray and I saw him walking in the hall and called to him but he did not hear me (I thought) and just walked by to the nurses' station. But the doctors had told him to come and see him first since they did not know if the baby was going to live. Then finally everything was OK and I was moved to the room with the other women.

We were several women in a large room and I met some other women from Germany and was happy to be able to speak with someone who spoke my own language. Our babies were in the room with us and we had to get up and feed them and another German woman next to me was very helpful. She had three children already and had been here longer than I had and could understand the language better.

Later Ray and I lived close to this lady on the base and we became good friends. Ray was gone a lot and I could not drive and so I walked everywhere I needed to go. The commissary was not far away and I went there often to get things I needed. There was a phone booth outside and when we wanted to go somewhere and needed a taxi, I would lift up the receiver and tell the person that I wanted a taxi and one would come and take me where I wanted to go on post for only 25 cents.

Before our son was born, I had tried to teach Carmen (16 months old) that she had to sleep in our bed since the new baby had to sleep in her bed. She did not like it and tried to pull him out of the bed after he came home. I was horrified when I saw what she had done; thankfully he was not injured and quickly got over the pain he obviously felt when she tried to pull him out through the wooden bars. After this incident, we bought a little car bed to put him in. Ray's father and mother came to visit and we rented another little cabin so they could sleep there.

One thing that I had never seen in Germany was roaches, but they seemed to be everywhere and we had to move several times because of them. When I got up in the night to fix a bottle for the baby and turned on the light, there went many roaches scurrying across the floor. They were everywhere and I felt sick to my stomach every time I saw them.

We lived in a trailer at that time off post, and it was getting cold and damp and both my children became very ill with pneumonia and had to be admitted to the hospital on post. Soon they were better and I took them home. My friend the German lady I met in the hospital told me that I should call the housing office on post and ask if I could get a better place than the one we lived in because my children were getting sick all the time.

At first I was reluctant to call since I thought they would not understand me, but finally I did and talked to a Col. Borman who was very helpful and arranged for me to move to a trailer on post. He even got a soldier to drive my loaded car, since I could not drive, and away we went to our new home. My husband was away on maneuvers in Louisiana at the time and did not know of our move. I had his address and would write to him, but with my limited vocabulary I wondered if he really would know where we were. When he returned, he had to find us and when he saw his car parked in front of the trailer he knew he was in the right place.

After Fort Leonard Wood, we were stationed in Fort Carson, Colorado. It was here that I met several German ladies with whom I wanted to be friends but my husband said I could not associate with them because they were all married to black soldiers. In those days black soldiers with white wives were never stationed in any of the southern states and therefore lots of them where in Fort Carson. It really did not make any difference to me since I had never seen black people until the Americans came and I did not understand what it was all about, but since my husband said I should not associate with them, I just did as I was told.

We lived in a trailer park and one day when I put my wash outside on the clothesline a sandstorm came and filled my wash with sand. Some clothes were blown away by the strong wind. We lived there long enough for me to get my American citizenship and after a year we moved back to Germany (it was 1956). We lived in Bad Kreuznach until 1960 and then moved to Fort Gordon, Georgia. Then on to Fort Benning, where we were living when my husband returned from Viet Nam. After this, we went back to Germany to Mannheim and were not long there when he had to go back to Viet Nam and we had 30 days to get out of our quarters and move. I decided to stay in Germany with the children and get a job, and moved not far away from where my family lived. My job was in the PX in Wiesbaden and we stayed there until Ray came back from Vietnam and was again stationed in Germany. But as soon as he was settled, he got orders to go back to Vietnam, which meant that the children and I would be alone again in Germany for at least 13 months. This is not what I had expected when I married Ray, and life was very different from the life I had seen my parents and grandparents live.

After this tour we lived in San Diego and my husband decided to get out of the Army in 1972. Jobs were hard to find and he finally got one working in a business that installed televisions in motels and hotels. At that time, people were not inclined to hire retired Vietnam veterans and so he had to work for minimum wages. Since he was so disgusted with the government at that time, he did not want to send his resume in for a job with any government agency. It was only after his sister told him that he should maybe try to get a civil service job at North Island, just up from San Diego, he actually applied and was hired right away. During our stay in California, our daughter was married, a happy occasion for all of us.

Unfortunately, our son was killed in a motorcycle accident. Needless to say, we were in severe shock and dismay. He was a young army sergeant, a medic, and was just accepted for training at Walter Reed as a physicians' assistant. While stationed in Grafenwoer, Germany he once delivered a baby at the dispensary. An American woman came in and the doctor on duty just happened to be out for lunch and that baby did not wait for him to return. So my son delivered the baby before the ambulance came to take her to the hospital. He was just under 25 years old.

Ray's job took us first to Utah and then to St.Louis and then to Luxemburg (which I did not like at all) and finally back to Germany where we lived first in Kaiserslautern and then Zweibruecken. By this time, Ray had about 18 years with civil service and wanted to stay until he had 20 years service time. Unfortunately, he began to have heart problems. He had to go for tests to Walter Reed Army Hospital and then back to Germany. But after a while it was determined at the Landstuhl Hospital that he had to have heart surgery and that was only done in the states. So we went on the medevac plane that left once a week from Landstuhl to Walter Reed and Ray had his by-pass surgery. The doctors then told him he could not resume his work in Germany anymore and so Ray retired from Civil Service. We moved to Florida first and to Arizona where the climate was more beneficial to us. Here Ray had serious back surgery from which he never really recovered.

Our daughter Carmen came to visit us there and suggested that maybe we should move back east again near Montgomery, AL where she lived. We did not like the VA hospital there and decided to look into moving to Decatur, Ga. where there was a good VA facility and a retirement community where we could move. The VA hospital was visited very often by Ray and the one thing I did not like was that the doctor would not let me go into the room with my husband. They were not very friendly in my opinion and so we decided to look for another place to go.

In the interim, our daughter had moved to Ardmore, TN. and we decided to move closer to her and her family. The VA hospital we wanted to use was in Nashville and after consideration of a few other places; we finally decided to settle in Columbia, TN. and to live in a very nice trailer community. Our daughter and her husband joined us a little later and now we lived just across the street from each other, which was a very pleasant arrangement. But one night Ray was not feeling well and did not want me to take him to the hospital. But after a while he relented and said "Ok take me to the hospital". By then it was midnight and I had just had cataract surgery and my night driving was difficult.

However, we made it to the hospital and I ran in at the emergency entrance to tell them my husband was sick and to get him out of the car. All the time I was driving, I did not know if he was alive or dead. I have no memory of how I made it safely to the hospital considering my eyesight problems and the stress of Ray's illness. After they admitted my husband to a room, I slumped into a wheelchair close by; a doctor came to me and thought I was the one that was ill and had just came in. I must have looked the part of someone in severe need of attention. However, after he examined my husband, he said that Ray had suffered a heart attack and that a stent should be installed. That is the protocol they administered and my husband lived without problems for an additional 15 months. One evening he went to bed and died during the night of a massive heart attack. There was no indication at the time that he had a medical emergency because he said that evening that he felt well. We had even made plans to go shopping the next day.

My life goes on and I will stay where I am and enjoy my family and endeavor to live each day to the fullest extent possible.

Hildegard & David

Rose

Christa & family

Kassel Wilhelmshöhe

Ray & Helga

Maria's Ragdoll

Kassel, Germany, after extensive bombing

Bobby & Margret in front of Rathaus

Margret

Uncle Helmut in Russia

Kassel rebuilt

Christel

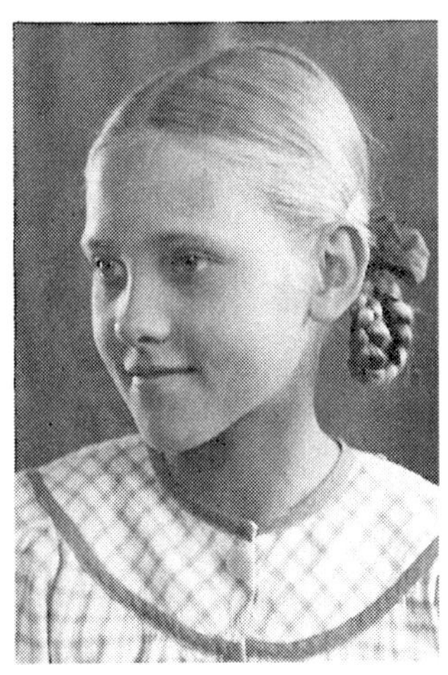

Monika

Brigitte

Chapter 6
MARIA

My father, Friedrich Simon, was born in the city of Trier on the Mosel in April 1903. My mother, Maria Lauer, was born in Otzenhausen (Hunsrück-Eifel), a farming village about 30.5 km (19 miles) from Trier. They met and were married in 1930, in Trier. My sister, Anita, was born in 1931; my brother Anton, was born in 1932; and I was born in 1934. As a child I saw and heard many things during the war that I did not understand. I did not comprehend much of what happened until I became an adult. These are some of my recollections during the war years.

I can remember as far back as the age of four, about 1938. Life was peaceful during this time. I went to kindergarten, which I now realize was more like a babysitting service than a learning facility. It was a short walk to kindergarten and I walked there by myself. I attended school from about 1940 to 1944 when we were evacuated from Trier. Before my father was drafted, jobs in Germany were scarce. He had worked for the French Foreign Legion where he learned to speak fluent French.

My father was drafted into the Wehrmacht in 1939. This was Hitler's Army, the unified armed forces of Nazi Germany (~1935 to 1945).

Resisting or evading the draft was punished by death. My father worked for a general, translating French to German. My father never told the authorities that he had worked for the French Foreign Legion because he was afraid they would have condemned him as a traitor. Before we were evacuated, my father was on military leave twice, for short periods of time. Upon one return from leave, my dad brought me two small French dolls. One was a little 3 ½-inch rag doll which I still have today.

During 1940, I can still remember spending much time playing outside mostly in a neighborhood park behind our apartment on Weberbach Straβe. We lived on the 4th floor of the apartment building. Our apartment had one bedroom and a kitchen and no other rooms. The landlady, Frau Ente, lived on the first floor. We only took a bath once a week. My mother boiled water on an old fashioned stove and poured a mixture of the boiling water and cold water into a cauldron for bathing.

On the second floor of our apartment building, an elderly lady named Frau Fromm lived with her grown son. Frau Fromm's son hated the Nazis. One day, the Gestapo came and took her son away. I remember the shouting. I heard that the son had said something criticizing the Nazis, which was not allowed. We never saw or heard anything about him again. My mother had a Jewish girlfriend that she and I sometimes visited. I eventually learned that Hitler hated the Jews and they were being rounded up. One day my mother told me that her girlfriend was taken away because she was Jewish.

Around 1942, food became scarce. Everyone received ration cards and we could only buy certain foods, and only for a week at a time. The state rationed milk and milk products, meat, sugar, marmalade, coffee, potatoes, eggs, dried goods, flour, bread, etc. A ration card was issued for each member of the family. Eventually because of the shortage of food, I was sent to the city of Allgäu to an Erholungsheim, a kind of rest home for undernourished children.

At first my home town of Trier was not attacked. The allied forces went to the larger cities, attacking bridges, factories, and railroad stations. I could hear the planes, the wailing sirens, and the bombs exploding in the distance. I don't remember what year it was when the allied bombing started. I do remember the terrifying sounds of sirens. At the first sighting of allied planes, the Voralarm (precaution alarm) was sounded. This alarm had a distinct sound; it indicated that enemy planes were on the way. After this alarm, the Vollalarm (air raid alert) was sounded; it had a different sound. This alarm meant that people had best be in their cellars. The final Entwarnung siren sounded an all clear, which indicated it was safe to leave the cellars.

Our cellar entrance was on the first floor of the apartment building behind the front door. The cellar's two doors were heavy steel with handles that could be opened only by an adult. Once the doors were open, there were eight steps down to the cellar. All buildings had small damp stone cellars separated one from another by a thick brick wall. An axe hung on the wall and in the event that you became trapped in your cellar, you could use the axe to knock down the wall and enter your neighbor's cellar.

Around the end of 1943, the air raid warnings came almost daily. My dad was in the military during this time and my mom was the sole caretaker for us three children. I was nine years old. The alarms usually sounded with very short notice and I could hear the planes approaching in the distance. We often went to bed fully dressed so that we would be ready to run to the cellar when the sirens blared. When the sirens sounded, my mom and we three kids grabbed clothes and blankets and ran, only God knows how quickly, down four flights of stairs (about 40 steps down) and into the cellar. One unforgettable air attack came when my brother had pneumonia. His fever was extremely high, and he could not stand up. My mother half-carried him down those 40 steps into the cellar.

In the spring of 1944, the city of Trier asked people to evacuate. My mother had filled a large trunk with valuables that she hoped to save while we were gone. She placed this in our cellar but unfortunately we would never see this trunk again. The house was later looted and what little we had was gone. When we evacuated, we could only take what we could carry in order to board a crowded train to a small farming village in the state of Thüringen. I was 9 ½ years old, my brother was 12, and my sister was 13.

The small farming village had only one grocery store. All the farmers were forced to take in refugee families such as ourselves. The farmer to whose home we were assigned resented this intrusion and was not compassionate toward us. My mother and the three of us were very much disliked. The farmer gave us one room that contained a small stove and we all had to sleep on mattresses on the floor. The ration cards provided very little food and we were always hungry. In retrospect, I admire my mother for her fierce will to survive and to keep her children fed. She ensured that we always had something to eat. Often, at dawn, we all went quietly out the house to the farmer's field where we stole potatoes, peas, carrots, and whatever else we could find. My mother did not define this as stealing. She considered this necessary to survive (note: Rightfully so! Maslow documented many years earlier that this is normal human behavior). The farm family had plenty of food, but inexplicably chose to share very little with us.

The farmer fed his cows and pigs Runkelrüben (rutabaga). My mother used this to make coffee by cutting it up in little squares, roasting it in the oven, and then brewing it. We all drank this coffee. The reluctant farm family had two cows, as well as some pigs, geese, and chickens. They once slaughtered a pig in the front yard and cooked the pork and made sausage, but they never shared any of this with us. The farmer had two children, a son and daughter. The son was about 23 years of age and the farmer made his son do all the dirty work on the farm. His tasks included cleaning out the filthy animal stalls. He also loaded pig manure, cow manure, and human waste onto a wheelbarrow and dumped this into an underground tank. The daughter was a privileged darling who never had to work.

In the small village there was a baking oven where on certain days the farmers baked bread. We did have bread to eat, although I don't remember how my mother was able to provide this for us. Time went by and there were no more air raids, or wailing sirens in the village. At this time there were no clothes or shoes to buy. My shoes were in bad shape in the winter of 1944, and I suffered severe frost bites on both heels and knees which caused me to miss school often. In the following spring, when the weather was warm, I made my own sandals from pieces of cardboard. I hand-sewed two strips of fabric, in a criss-cross pattern, across the cardboard so my feet would fit into these homemade shoes. They did not last very long.

Around D-day, in 1945, we received news that Germany had lost the war. Russian soldiers started to come through the villages going from house to house, looking for men and for food. The farmer's son was taken away by the Russians. My mother was about 40 at this time, and my sister was 14. Both were terribly afraid of the Russians and had heard news of Russian soldiers raping German women in other villages. Fortunately my family did not suffer any of these unspeakable atrocities.

After the Russians, the American soldiers came through the village. They also went from house to house, looking for food. The Americans asked for eggs (this seemed to be one of the few German words they knew). The state of Thüringen became part of the Russian Occupied Zone. We had not heard from my father since we evacuated Trier. I don't know how my father found us, but he did. I will never forget that moment because I saw him first. I happened to look out the front window one day, and I saw him. "There comes papa!" I screamed. My mother, sister, and brother looked out the window to see if this was so. My father had come to get us. It was the happiest moment I had felt in a very long time. I never asked him how he found us. Previous to finding us, my father went to our home town, found a small apartment, and bought furniture for it. He had prepared a home for us. My dad had been taken prisoner by the Americans in the spring of 1945, and was released by the summer of the same year. The Americans kept German soldiers who were high ranking officers but they soon released the ordinary soldiers because they knew they had been forced to serve.

Death was the only alternative to serving Adolph Hitler. My father never supported the dictatorial regime of Adolph Hitler.

Because we were in the Russian Zone of Germany, we needed to return to the west, back to Trier. Eventually we were able to quietly sneak out of the Russian zone. On our first try, we left one night at dusk, taking only what each of us could carry. My dad had a plan, and tried to remember the way. This first night we were unsuccessful; my dad had miscalculated the directions and in the darkness we could not find our way. After walking for a long time, we came to a hill; but by then it was pitch dark. Suddenly, my dad made us all lie down, and I saw why. On top of the hill were two Russian soldiers standing, talking to each other. They did not see us so we stayed crouched down, and slowly made our way back to the farm house.

On the second night, we made it to a village that was occupied by the Russians. As we walked by a street, we were caught by a Russian officer on a horseback. He stopped us and spoke in halted German to my dad. My dad showed him the release papers from the Americans. I think this officer felt sorry for us because we probably looked very pitiful. The officer took the papers from my dad and told him to come to the station, and then he left us alone; he probably knew we would not come. As soon as the officer was gone, my dad asked a family nearby to take us in for one night, which they did. In return, my mother had to give this family the three quilts we had. Sadly, no one ever did anything for free.

The next day, we took a train to Trier and went to the apartment my dad had for us. After settling in the new apartment, we visited what was left of our old apartment. What we saw confirmed that our evacuation was the right choice; our old apartment had taken a direct hit from a bomb. The bomb went all the way through to the cellar. Had we been in that cellar, we would not have survived. Most of the building's walls, the stairs, etc., were a pile of rubble; only one wall remained. We looked up to the small section that was left of our fourth floor room. On the edge of what little flooring remained, my brother's nightstand was perched. It was all that remained. Recently, I learned that 23 December 1944 was "Trier Black Day;" when 700 tons of munitions and mines were dropped in the area of my home town[1].

My father found a job as a laborer, which did not pay much money. Food was still very scarce, and the food shortage lasted about two years. The ration cards enabled us to get sugar, flour, margarine, and some other things. We got one loaf of bread per person, per week. Each loaf was sliced into seven pieces and we ate only one slice of bread each day.

I remember being hungry most of the time. It seemed as if my family was always hungry. In these lean days, we had some fish, and we had Salzkartoffeln, or salt potatoes. My mom used to make a gravy sauce from flour, beef bouillon, and spices. As beef bouillon could not be found during these times, and flour was rationed, we only had plain potatoes with salt. Salt was the only available flavoring for food. Milk was also rationed. Infants were permitted a certain amount of whole milk each day and the older children were allowed only a certain amount of skim milk each day. Many city people walked or took a train to villages that had more food. The purpose was to trade some goods for food. My mom made these trips frequently and she always took me along. I think she did this so that the farmers would feel sorry for us, because I looked very malnourished. When we had nothing to trade, we begged for food. Sometimes we got a piece of bread; sometimes we got an egg, flour, or even a piece of bacon. Once, my dad brought home a rabbit, and slaughtered it in the kitchen. When I saw all the insides, I could not eat a bite of that rabbit.

The butcher shops sold only horsemeat on certain days. So people lined up about two hours before the shop opened to get some meat. There were always long lines and long waits at the grocery stores. This was normal and my mom, sister, and I stood in these long lines for years. Farmers also came to town to sell their potatoes. When possible, we bought potatoes in 100-lb sacks. We ate a lot of potatoes during these years. Mom and I often collected fruit and nuts in the summer. We had a big forest nearby that had wild blueberries growing in it. Wild blackberry and raspberry bushes, as well as hazelnut bushes, also grew along the fields. My mom made marmalade from this fruit that we had gathered. Mom made salads from the wild bitter dandelion leaves. Bitter or not, it was food. Clothing was also hard to find so my mother sewed clothes for us. She knitted us shawls, socks, and sweaters. She once even knitted a panty for me. I hated that itchy, uncomfortable garment.

There were trucks that brought and sold coal to families for ovens/ stoves. From this source we were able to buy coal briquettes for the ovens. These large briquettes burned all night and provided heat for the kitchen. Our bedrooms did not have heat.

Trier was occupied by French soldiers. The French soldiers took the best houses in the city for themselves and their families. In one of the streets was a Villa, a large residence with a fence all around it. The German owners had to move out so that high-ranking French officers could move in. The French soldiers treated the Germans in a very condescending manner. If a German man came across a French official, the German had to step off the curb to let the Frenchman go by.

My father was a very stressed and nervous man and he smoked frequently to calm his nerves. In the bad years, cigarettes were scarce. My father made my brother and me go into the streets to pick up cigarette butts that we found next to the curbs and bring these to him. He opened these discarded used butts and removed the tobacco to roll his own cigarettes. When these were smoked and my father had no more, my brother and I returned to the streets. My brother and I were very embarrassed to do this.

With the Währungsreform (currency reform) in 1948, citizens lost money from the transition of the Reichsmark to the Deutsche Mark. We received only 10% from the amount we exchanged. Food and supplies became more plentiful though and the rationing stopped. My dad got a better job, working for the French Government as a translator. With this employment, we had the privilege of going to the French commissary to buy food; foods and fruits that I had never seen before. My dad could also buy cigarettes here.

I went back to school in 1945, and completed the mandatory 8 years of schooling required under German law in 1948. For about two years, the school served one meal a day to schoolchildren. Meals consisted of grits boiled in milk with prunes (which I hated), or coco with brötchen, my favorite. After this, I took a trade, working under contract for three years, and going to trade school once a week. My parents wanted me to work and I had to take the first job available, which was to learn to be a grocer. I did not like this because I always wanted to be a tailor. In those days, parents made such choices for their children. I worked extremely hard during these 3 years, from 1950 to 1953, riding my bicycle about 5 miles to a warehouse that sold fruits and vegetables. At the warehouse, I loaded 100 lb of produce onto the hanger attached to my bicycle, and made the 5-mile ride back to the grocery store. It took all the strength in my 15½-year old, 100-lb, 5'2" frame to pedal back to the grocery store.

The grocery store was located near a mountain that was accessed by climbing stairs in the side of the mountain. A few customers lived in houses beside the stairs on the way up the mountain. These customers ordered their food from the grocery store and we trainees had to carry about 50 lb of groceries to them, on foot. The mountain was steep; I always had to rest a few times on the way up. As food items were not packaged like they are today, individual grocery items had to be weighed and the cost calculated. We didn't have an adding machine so I manually calculated food costs and wrote prices on a piece of paper. I also had to visit customers to collect money they owed for items they had bought on credit and had not paid when the bill was due. The three years I spent in this trade, from 1950 to 1953, was all manual labor and very little learning. In my first year, I received 25 DM per month. My income in the second year was 35 DM a month, and in the third year, 45 DM a month and I had to give part of this to my parents. After these three years, I worked for an accountant in a grocery warehouse and I liked this job very much.

After the war (1948 or 1950), relatives told me some very sad news about a young cousin, who was playing in the fields in Otzenhausen.

A half-buried bomb exploded when my 14-year old cousin stepped on it and he was killed. In 1961 I met my American husband, who was stationed in the area. We married in April 1962, and I entered the U.S. in October 1962. My father died of lung cancer at the age of 62; my mother lived to the age of 94.

[1] Friedrich, Jörg (April 7, 2008), *The Fire: The Bombing of Germany, 1940–1945*, Columbia University Press, ISBN-10: 0231133812, ISBN-13: 978-0231133814.

Chapter 7
MONIKA

I was born in Ludwigshafen, Germany in 1936, and my parents were living in Karlsruhe where my father was busy writing his theses for his PhD. After that we moved to Kiel where my brother Christoph was born in 1939. My father worked in the war industry building submarines for the German government. We lived there until 1942, when father was transferred to southern Germany, to Neckarsulm. So before leaving, all our furniture was put in storage in Kiel and we moved away, only to get the news shortly thereafter that a bomb had hit the storage facility and destroyed all the contents. We have a picture where my mother stands next to the burned out building holding some little burned toy in her hand and my little silver cup that did not get sent away. Of course the silver was all melted and one could scarcely make out what it was before.

Only a few valuable items like the silver and some pictures were sent to the grandparents in Stettin, and these items survived. In Neckarsulm, my dad worked with Karl Schmitt on the design of turbines. That is all I can remember being talked about, but it was a war related job as much of the other industry in the area. We lived in a little town called Jagstfeld until 1952.

My grandparents had a large clothing store in Stettin; supplying the sea trade with items of clothing and other items one needs on ships. My aunt and her husband owned a large restaurant there also. Since my grandfather was originally from Sweden, he and grandmother went back there after their business was destroyed by Russian bombing. For a long time we did not know what had happened to them, as was the case with many families fleeing from that area of eastern Germany to escape the Russians. The area we lived in was relatively peaceful and only on a few occasions a plane would come over and drop one bomb. But then in 1944 there was an attack on Heilbronn, about 25 miles away, and we saw the fires in the sky and heard the bombers fly overhead.

The bombing of larger cities continued until early 1945 but not in our immediate area. When the sirens sounded the alarm and the planes were on their way, no one knew just where they would drop their load of bombs and so we had to seek shelter and that was very scary. The sound of hundreds of planes overhead is a terrifying experience for anyone. We all had to go to a shelter, because there was a lot of shooting and it was not safe to be out on the streets.

At first there were tanks and German troops to defend the town "to the last man" as was the order. But little by little they left and their vehicles also withdrew. Father and a few others were ordered by the SS to defend the little town but as soon as the German troops left, father and the others put out a white flag because the Americans were just across the river. Everyone knew that if the German troops came back, all the men who put that white flag out would be shot. This was true, but thank God the Germans did not come back.

Once, soon after we had been in the shelter, there was a big commotion and we heard trucks and tanks coming down the streets and when we looked, there were the Americans. We saw black soldiers for the first time in our lives. I was nine years old and remember it well and how surprised I was.

My friends and I had never seen black people before, only in pictures.

They were very friendly, helping my mother put the big carpet on the rack outside where it got a good beating before being put into the house again. My father spoke some English and was able to converse with the men and it was not long before one of the soldiers asked my dad to help him find a wife!

After some time the black soldiers moved on and were replaced by white American soldiers. The soldiers gave us little candies that looked like M&M's and of course we were happy.

Our apartment was built onto a hotel and the American army took that entire building. As soon as they arrived, they came to our apartment and told us we had one hour to get out, they needed the apartment! What to take and what not was a big decision. We moved in with friends as that was our only option. My brother was suffering from severe bronchitis and it was good that we only stayed there for about two weeks when we were able move back into our apartment again. But what a surprise awaited us! The place was filthy; furniture and other objects were broken; father's books were gone as was his film equipment and many other items. But at least we were back in our own apartment.

My father soon found work again with an architect and together they designed a bridge which was quickly built, because many bridges had been destroyed during the war. I don't remember ever going hungry because we were very lucky that there was always something to eat. In the summer there was a lot of fruit and sometimes someone said "There is a lot of cabbage to be had in Munich" and we hopped on the train and went there. My mother baked bread and we also received care packages.

After the war my grandparents, who were in Sweden, found out where we were and were able to send us many good things to eat which were lacking in Germany at that time. Coffee and Tea and other things could be traded for potatoes and other necessities. Also, mother went early in the morning into the forest and collected beech nuts that were then taken to town and oil was extracted which she used for cooking. There was always news of some kind such as: there is a train loaded with sugar beets or a load of Plexiglas, so we all took off to the train station to get as much as we could carry and brought it home. Sugar beets made the most delicious syrup which we all enjoyed eating.

Any meat that was to be obtained was reserved for father. One day my mother came home with something that she breaded and fried and father ate it before asking what was. She told him: "Cow udder!" Once we received an orange from our grandmother who lived in Nurnberg and my brother bit into it as if it was an apple.

The white Americans were not as generous with food gifts as were the black soldiers. However, once we were just walking along the road when an American truck came by and the soldiers threw out little packages which we took them home and discovered they were pressed cocoa. We had hot chocolate, real hot chocolate, at a time when such luxuries as that were unavailable in the German stores. As schoolchildren I also remember that we had to go out to the potato fields and pick off the potato bugs. The fields were guarded so that no potatoes could be stolen.

We also went to the Americans' kitchen at the hotel and the people working there gave us pineapple; a real treat since we never had anything like it before. During school days in war time, our classes were disrupted at times when the sirens sounded and we had to go to a shelter, but nothing really big ever happened in our town. The bomber squadrons usually went to the larger cities and dropped their bombs. Thankfully, we were spared the wholesale destruction that was evident in much of Germany.

In 1952 my father was offered a position as a professor of engineering at a school in Frankfurt and we moved there. Frankfurt had been heavily bombed and many houses were destroyed along with much of the infrastructure. But father was able to find a nice apartment across from a park and we moved there.

I started school studying to become a kindergarten teacher and finished two years later. While working as a teacher, I met one of my instructors from the college and she asked me if I would like to go to Venezuela as a nanny. The family in Venezuela had emigrated there from Germany (the father was a Jew and knew that to stay in Germany would have been a disaster for him and his family). So every two years, he hired a girl from the school to come and take care of his children. After I consulted with my father, he said he thought it was a good idea and so on my 20th Birthday I arrived in Caracas Venezuela. The family had another baby while I was with them which made a total of five children.

During my stay there, I met other German nationals and really enjoyed my time there. Once, another family mentioned that they also had hired a nanny from Frankfurt and it turned out to be a former classmate of mine. After two years it was time to go home again. For the return trip, I traveled on a freighter and the entire trip took six weeks. But it was a beautiful new ship from Germany and we made stops in Columbia and Cuba among many other places. After arriving back home I received another job offer in the Belgian Congo but had some time to think about it before I had to decide if I wished to go.

In 1959, my parents decided to take a vacation to the little town of Jagstfeld, where we lived during the war. We still had many friends there and I also met many of my old school friends. They invited me to go with them one weekend to a little place called "Die Backstube" (the baking room); a little place where young people meet and also Americans came. The place was a bakery and a restaurant. There was always someone playing a guitar and they had wonderful pastries. The owners were a couple who really enjoyed young people and many American soldiers came there because it was a friendly place.

Ben also was there at the time I came with my friends. He was friendly but I was not interested. Later that evening, I invited these friends to visit me in Frankfurt. When they came Ben came also. We all went out and danced and had a good time and got to know each other a little better. Ben went back to the base where he was stationed, but he left his record player behind (accidently on purpose I think). He returned soon and then came the serious question. He first asked my dad and we became engaged soon thereafter. We finally completed the paperwork to get married, which took several months to finalize. The fact that my mother was from Poland and I had lived in South America for two years complicated the processing for the Americans. At that time, the Americans investigated us as far back as possible before giving us permission to marry.

I spoke better Spanish than English and so our conversation did not include too many serious things. Our understanding of each other was limited. I would advise young people not to rush into marriage so soon, but to first get to know each other better. Our first duty station was Fort Bragg, North Carolina, and after we arrived and I saw the place, I was ready to return home to Germany immediately. I had a certain idea what America was like but to see it was really shocking. All I saw was gas stations and utility poles with wires all over the place. The place was not at all what I had imagined; it was rocky, dusty and not pretty at all.

When visiting my husband's family, I felt as if I had fallen into a beehive, there were so many people and not all were in attendance! What a shock! He was one of nine children! In1963 Ben received orders for Korea. Our son Tom was born in Germany and after my husband left for Korea, in August our second son Chris was born. At first I lived with my in-laws but since I wanted to stay on good terms with them, I knew I had to move to my own place. I wanted to raise my children my way and that was not possible in someone else's house. I prayed and asked God to help me find a good place and He did. It was a little duplex and I told my in-laws I will be glad if they visit, since I will not have a phone and I did not have a TV. They thought I would be bored, but with two children, one can scarcely be bored; besides I like to read and to do many things with the children.

I started going to a little Baptist Church and it certainly was new to me, so informal and different from the Lutheran churches in Germany. I liked the people there and God showed me through preaching that I was a sinner and needed a Savior and so I became a Christian. It was a most enjoyable year. When Ben came home in '64 he saw his second son Chris, who was almost a year old, for the first time.

Our next duty station was Germany and I was so happy to see my family again. After 3 years in Germany, we went back to the states and Ben received orders for Viet Nam, and I went back to Shelbyville, Tennessee. After Viet Nam, we went back to Germany for three years and then we came to Huntsville, AL. After this duty station, we went to Italy and then back here to Huntsville where Ben retired from the Army in 1976.

We moved to Shelbyville where Ben found a position in sales. The boys were in school and I did not want to be home alone. I was accustomed to being around people doing things, so I started working with handicapped children. In the summers when school was out, I went back to Germany to visit my parents. Once, when I was ready to go to Germany, Ben said he heard about a gas station that was for sale and he wanted to look into it. I told him if he bought it to call me because I was not coming back.

I got a call one day in Germany telling me to change my ticket to Chicago. He had a job in Illinois and had moved everything there already. Praise God! The place was Zion, right next to Lake Michigan and in a beautiful little town. I was thinking that perhaps I might be able to put roots down right here.

After about three years the company boss said that he did not like Christians and Ben decided that he did not have to tolerate that. He called a contact in Spartanburg, North Carolina and asked if they needed someone to work there. They did. So we moved there and I was able to work in a school for handicapped children for four years. We attended a church there for a while and then decided that it did not feel just right for us. I looked for another church and prayed. When we first moved into the apartment I saw a little church close by and that is where I went. After hearing the pastor preach, I knew this was the right church and I started attending there. This church had all the things I wanted to be involved in, i.e. children's ministries and nursing home visits. After a while Ben came to church also.

The city of Spartanburg was very beautiful and I would like to have remained there, but our children and grandchildren were here in Madison, AL. We were getting older and we decided to retire and come here in 2002. We now attend Providence Baptist Church and are happy there. On Wednesday night we meet in homes and after a certain time we switch groups and thereby get to know everyone who comes to church.

Both of my brothers are still living in Germany. Christoph lives in Hamburg where he is an artist. He displays his works in many galleries in Europe. Lorenz is married, and is a law professor and psychoanalyst with his own office.

Chapter 8
BRIGITTE

I was born in 1942, in Pershkin, a small town close to Königsberg in East Prussia. When you look at a map of Germany it is located in the northeast. My parents were Margret and Emil Orlowski, and I had an older sister and brother, Christel, and Siegfried. Our father was in the German Army in France during that time and was not at home when I was born. He was able to come later when I was crawling and that was the only time he ever saw me, according to my mother. After he visited on leave, he had to go to the eastern front, Russia, where he died.

After I was one year old, the government issued an order for all German-speaking people to be forcibly evacuated because of the threat of Russian soldiers occupying the area. Anyone who did not comply was in danger of being shot. Other people had already packed up all they could carry and left the area; but I think my mother did not want to leave in case father came back. Many families were lost during that time; some by starvation on the way south or west and some were overtaken by the Russians and were killed, or worse. The weather was a big factor also; there was not enough shelter and warmth, so many people froze to death, sadly mostly the children and young infants. So my mother, grandmother and brother and sister and I were put in cattle cars, and the trains moved south. We had nothing but the clothes on our backs, a little food and our identification papers and a few pictures that were lost later in our travels.

The train cars were so packed that people hardly had room to turn and there were no bathroom facilities to use. Several elderly people died. Conditions were most unsanitary. Once the train stopped because there was an air raid and all the people had to leave the train and go to a shelter. In the confusion, my grandmother was lost and we never knew what happened to her, since we were herded back to the train after the attack was over, and the train continued on. To think of the grief my mother must have felt and the helpless state she was feeling, is almost impossible to comprehend. My brother Siegfried was five at that time and my sister Christel was nine. Mother told me that during that time people washed the children's hair with black coffee so they would not get lice or they hoped that the coffee would kill the lice if they were present.

Mother said the only thing the authorities told them was that the train was going south. How far, no one knew. But finally, after days of these miserable conditions, we arrived in the München (Munich) area where we were quartered forcibly with a farm family outside the city. I say forcibly because we were refugees without resources and many people did not like their lives disrupted by strange people having to live in their houses. However, the home owners had no choice because the authorities had earlier surveyed all the houses and knew of any available space. We were simply assigned space with this uncooperative farm family. The owners of some apple trees nearby even objected to us gathering up apples that had fallen from the trees. Conditions were primitive; we had no heat in the room where we lived, and it was winter by this time. We were all sick and my mother, having no other recourse, went to the local Catholic home for children, and asked them if they would take us since she had no means to provide for us. It was a time of extreme suffering for the population at large, but especially for those who had the misfortune of no home, no husband and no money.

She was told that since we were Protestant, we would have to be raised in the Catholic faith and our names were to be changed also. I became Theresa, my brother was to be call Joseph and my sister was renamed Maria. Mother then found work as a domestic for a family that was more fortunate.

Mother told me that after the Americans came she found work for a Colonel and his family. They treated her very well and she was considered a member of their family. She cooked and washed and cleaned and did everything she knew how to do. And she always came to see us on Sundays; it was a day we looked forward to very much.

In later years, my sister and I understood why mother had to put us in the Catholic home, it was clearly to save our lives and we understood that she did the very best for us that she could, considering the circumstances. We also knew that she loved us and was never happy about the separation. But our brother never agreed with us and said somehow she could have done better. He never really explained to us exactly what she should have done. My sister and I were devastated by his treatment of mother and we have never spoken with him again and remain estranged until this day. About ten years later, mother remarried and had three more children. I was able to get to know the oldest boy quite well but not the other boy and girl since they were much younger.

I left school at 14, and mother told me that when she looked across the street into the school room window, she saw that I was walking around teaching the children and thought if I did that I must be pretty smart; so she took me out of that school and put me into another school, the equivalent of a high school. But there the young people were from affluent families and I did not feel very welcome there. They all had nice clothes to wear and went to places I knew nothing about and I just did not feel comfortable there at all. So I quit school and went to work because I clearly needed the money. My first job was in a factory.

It was during this time that my older sister Christel was engaged to be married to a German man and the wedding was to be on a Sunday. On the day before, (Saturday), her fiancé visited with her and got on his motorcycle, waved good bye and was hit by a truck; his head severed and thrown across the street by the impact. My sister saw it all and was so traumatized that she was never the same. Now we know she should have been under a doctor's care and maybe that would have helped her, but at that time no one ever thought of that. There were times after this that mother and I would not see her for two weeks at a time and we had no idea where she was. But then someone would tell mother that they saw Christel somewhere and I took a train or bus and went to wherever she was to bring her back.

Once someone told mother that they had seen my sister in such and such a place in Kaiserslautern. I took the train and went to the Gasthaus where my sister was, and I was standing next to the juke box, when an American soldier asked if I would like to play a song; it was Jerry, who was to be my future husband. I replied in the little English I knew, that I did not care one way or the other. So that was that and I proceeded to take my sister home.

In the meantime, my mother found me a job in Kaiserslautern as an errand girl for a lawyer. The arrangement also included a room in the lawyer's house and I would do housework for them on days when they did not need me at the office.

Sometime later I was standing at a bus stop in Kaiserslautern when an American soldier stopped and told me that Jerry was looking for me. What a surprise, since I had forgotten about that soldier and was busy with my work and was dating other German boys. I saw Jerry again and we dated and when I took him to meet my mother, she did not like him because he was too quiet; he just did not talk a lot. She said I should find one that was more fun to be around; this one was no fun. I liked Jerry well enough though and kept dating him. I really was attracted to him because he was sort of mysterious and I could never quite figure him out. He presented a challenge. With some people you know after a while who they are and a lot about them, but not Jerry. It was as if he had a veil of secrecy surrounding himself. After a while, mother got used to him and she did not mind if I went around with him. We really only went to a Gasthaus and sat and listened to the music, and otherwise the outing with him could be boring. But things moved right along and then came the day when Jerry said that he had to leave and go back to the States. He just did not want to re-enlist and stay in Germany. We decided that after he left in 1959, I would get my papers together and join him in Athens, Alabama.

That is exactly what we did and we were married at the Athens, AL Courthouse in 1960. By then Jerry had gotten out of the Army and was looking for a job, but was unable to get what he wanted. Finally he decided to go back into the Army. We lived in Fort Benning, GA a while and our second child was born there. Now we had a son and a daughter. We lived there about three years and then went back to Germany, to Babenhausen. In Germany, we had another girl who was born in Frankfurt. After moving around for several years I was happy to go to Germany again.

My mother was happy to see my children and to see that I was well and happy with my life. Our time in Germany was three years and then we came to Redstone Arsenal, where Jerry was stationed for about seven years. Our children have grown up, of course, and are married. However, tragically one of our daughters died.

After thirty years in the Army Jerry retired, and we have lived in the Athens area ever since. We are happy in our retirement and expect to remain here.

Chapter 9
MISCELLANEOUS

Some individuals could only provide very short accountings of their childhood in Germany during the war and the years immediately afterwards. Perhaps this was because over time memories had dimmed or perhaps there was an overpowering sense that some things were too personal and too horrifying to recount. These short accountings are collected here in this miscellaneous chapter. All this information is worthy of documentation, because this was not something that occurred in the very distant past, but these horrifying events all happened within the memory of currently living individuals.

Elisabeth

My entire family including all relatives close and not so close, lived in the city of Boesing-Pezinok, east of Bratislava, at the foot of the Smaller Carpatian Mountains in Slowakia. Bratislava is the Capitol city and is 65 kilometers away from Vienna, Austria. We all were farmers and grew grapes for wine. We had a German Church and School in Boesing.

The Russians Arrive

The day the Russian soldiers came to our area we were living with my grandfather on my father's side. It was in the spring of 1945 and the family was at the Grandparent Fakundiny's home. That particular day, my grandfather gave me a message to take to an elderly lady about a delivery of some wood. My brother Willi went along with me. He was about five years old and I was eight. We knew the lady very well, and I had visited her often. The owner of the house where she lived had a beautiful dog and I enjoyed playing with him. Willi started begging to go home, but I was not ready since I loved playing with the dog. So our trip back home was delayed somewhat. Suddenly we heard loud explosions and shooting and we tried to run back to the grandparents' house. The owner of the house where we were visiting also heard the shooting and he shut the big gate leading into the apartment building. We screamed and pounded on that door until mother came through a break in the brick wall surrounding the houses. She snatched up my little brother and away we ran through the grape orchard with bullets flying over us, but we made it to our house without a scratch.

Occupation

One day after the Russian occupation began, our place was packed but all our neighbors were gone. Grandfather was getting feed for the horses and was cursing loudly in German. Nobody was supposed to know that we were German. When asked our names, we had to answer and say our names in Slovak. So my name was Alsbeta (instead of Elisabeth). It was easy for me, but my younger brother had to learn fast. Grandfather had given part of his house over to a Russian officer and his wife and because of that he was not molested by other unrestrained Russian soldiers who roamed through the streets stealing and plundering (or worse).

On this particular day, the family was gathered again at my grandparents' house. Earlier, the discussion had been that in case of bombing, the wine cellar was the safest place to be. It was built deep into the ground with large stones. I liked to go to the wine cellar. It had a smaller room on the right side before one went into the bigger cellar. There we had grapes hanging on a string in fall, and nice pears in large wheat boxes. Also, there were carrots stored in sand.

The Russians with their horses had settled down in and around our house and yard. As I stood among the Russians in the yard, planes came flying overhead. I remember seeing the heavy bombers. One Russian soldier said, "They are ours". At that moment, my grandmother called me into the house. Then it happened. There was a very loud explosion and we were all thrown to the floor. My grandmother was next to me and she grabbed my head and held me down. My thought was: THE WINE CELLAR! I struggled to get free from the hand of my grandmother and started running towards the door. I had to jump over wounded and dying Russian soldiers and their horses. I made it to the wine cellar safely and sat there waiting for the others to arrive. My family searched for me, not knowing that I was there waiting for them.

Later we found out that none of our family was injured, since everyone was in the house. A total of 3 bombs fell. One fell in front of our house, and one next door. Luckily no one next door was home at the time. The third bomb fell across the street and a young couple from Bratislava was killed. The couple had been staying with us, until an officer requested for them to return to their house. There were about 16 Russians dead and also 18 horses. A Russian officer came later and asked my father how many civilians were killed at our place. My father had to reply: "None".

After Slowakia came under Soviet Russian occupation, everything German had to be closed. Later, all the German speaking people were gathered up and marched on foot into a camp outside of the city. They were allowed to take nothing but the clothes on their backs. One day my grandmother took my little brother and me and we just walked out of the camp and went back home. Somehow the guards did not stop us. I remember going back to the camp every day with a container of milk for my mother. It was for my little sister and a baby brother.

Another day as I arrived at the gate, I was told that my mother was not in the camp anymore but had been sent to the one near Pressburg. I was very upset by this news and ran home crying. A short time later my grandmother and little brother and I were put into that same camp and we were together again. The parents and all able bodied people were required to work in the fields all day and the children just roamed around unattended. When the parents returned from working in the fields all day they sometimes brought home potatoes. I sliced mine and placed them on top of the large iron stove and to let them bake. They tasted very good compared to the meager camp food we received.

At times we heard that we would get paper and pencils and a school would be started, but it never happened. That was a big disappointment for me. When I finally started school, two years late, I could not even write the simplest word.

My grandmother again boldly took me and another little girl and went out of the camp to go back to her house in Boesing-Pezinok. It was winter and icy cold as we walked across a large bridge over the Danube River. Everything was frozen and when a Russian guard called to us, my grandmother was startled and fell, but he came over and helped her up and told her to be careful. From there we walked to the train station and caught a train back to Boesing-Pezinok.

Later we were forced back to the camp and all the people were put into cattle cars for a long ride to Germany. Conditions on the train were unimaginable, no sanitary facilities, only straw to lie down on and no heat. We were the lucky ones; we were sent to the American Occupation Zone; unfortunately my uncle and his family had to go to the Russian Zone.

Before we came west, our youngest brother died in the camp in Pressburg; he was only seven months old. There was no milk or suitable food available for infants and therefore most of them died as did the old people that were in the camp. My little pre-school sister just went around begging for food from other families and most gave her a little something from the meager portions they had, and that is how she was able to stay alive. (Note: As an adult, the realization that my baby brother starved to death in a refugee camp is still most unsettling. In a civilized ordered society, this is unimaginable. I can only surmise, sadly, that the prevailing conditions were so bleak that even though the authorities did all that they could, it was beyond their resources. I also realize that these conditions were not uncommon for the times. The pain for my parents must have been horrendous as they helplessly watched this occur.)

Eventually we lived in a refugee camp in Esslingen; it was a very nice place compared to where the Russians had earlier imprisoned us behind barbed wire. At Esslingen we were able to move around freely and that alone felt so wonderful. At Esslingen, mother saved our sugar ration stamps and traded them to the farmers nearby for potatoes and flour, with which she could cook a most wonderful meal. A homemade meal was always wonderful treat for us.

Later we were settled in the refugee camp in the town of Mettingen, a suburb of Esslingen. There my father was able to work for the town as a laborer and mother worked for a farmer in Mettingen. My siblings were younger than I and we all attended the schools in Mettingen and Esslingen

Epilogue

Eventually, I took a test to attend a trade school, but did not pass the examination, so at fourteen years of age I began to work in the city library. I was someone who did all things for all people. My employer wanted me to attend the school for library science, but one needed to finish High School for that and so I did not qualify.

I then decided to go to nursing school in Ulm because that did not cost anything and I really had my heart set on that profession. We would even receive a small amount of money, and other benefits such as housing and food were included. However, my parents did not want me to become a nurse; they said it was too much work for not enough pay. And since I was underage, I had to wait until I was twenty one and did not need my parents' permission. I was in the first class and it took me three years to finish. But finally I graduated and was hired immediately by the Hospital in Ulm, since nurses were desperately needed. Later I worked in the American Dispensary in Neu-Ulm where I met my husband.

As I look back at all the horrors of war, the violence, the evictions, refugee camps, and the stress of always trying to find food and housing, to this day I still envy people who have been fortunate enough to stay in the homes where they were born and grew up.

Christa

The town we lived in was Senftenberg, Germany. It was south, southeast of Berlin. I was born in Spremberg, 1936. With a promise of a better job for my father, we moved to Senftenberg when I was about six years old. All this fell through because father again refused to join the Nazi party as he had refused on previous occasions. For a short time, until he was drafted, he had a job with the Justice Department.

I was nine years old when World War II ended. I remember it like it was yesterday. The year before the war ended, going to school had not been easy. We always had to walk in the shadow side of the houses in case Allied airplanes flew over. Walking in the shadows made it harder for the pilots to spot us. Often the sirens went off and we had to take cover in entrances ways. When we were at school and the alarm sounded, we were taken down to the basement. At the age of nine, it was a game for me. The real thing came later.

I came from a large family, with three brothers and four sisters. My oldest brother was 22 years old and was already in Hitler's army and my oldest sister was in a labor camp "Arbeitdienst". Young ladies without training had to teach, work in hospitals, or babysit for mothers working for the government in military factories. My next brother was 16 and was drafted into an anti-aircraft Battery.

The last time our entire family was together was at my parent's 25th wedding anniversary. Shortly after, my oldest brother was killed in action. Most fathers with large families were allowed to stay home. My father, who as I earlier stated, refused to join the Nazi Party, was the oldest draftee in Germany. That left mother to care for all the children. We had to flee in the spring of 1945 after the bombing of our city. I remember our doll buggies were loaded with clothes and shoes, and our school backpacks were also filled.

We all had to report to the train station. There we were loaded into cattle cars and off we went. The cattle cars, of course had a fantastic aroma. We only made it about 40 miles from our city. The train tracks were destroyed by bombs and the Russians were faster than we. The next day, the Russians made us all start walking back the 40 miles to the city. We stayed about one year under Russia occupation before traveling to the West. Some of the people had wagons to carry their belongings, we had to carry our things and push buggies. We went over war torn roads where the night before a battle had raged. Many dead soldiers and animals were on the side of the road. At the time, it all went over my head, but later I can remember it all with great clarity.

Back home, the city was on fire. We found a place to stay outside of the city. We shared a villa with three other families. How my Mother and the two other ladies kept what was now 10 children fed, washed and clothed, is very hard to comprehend. Both of my brothers, with one bicycle between them, went to farms to beg for food and most often had to work all day for a small bag of potatoes or flour. At that time, there were no stores, so nothing could be bought even if we had money. Later in order to earn a little money, all of us made thousands of folded paper stars and sold them for Christmas tree ornaments. Later this money was used to pay for train tickets.

My father, who was captured earlier in the war, was released from the prisoner of war camp but was only allowed to stay in the West German sector that was under British occupancy. So whatever we could carry was packed up again and we tried to get across the border to the western part of Germany. We had official papers for all of us to leave but at every border crossing we were sent to the next one. We made it across the border to the west after about three or four closed crossings attempts.

When in West Germany, it was a lot easier to travel, but after not eating for two days, we were very hungry and still had a long way to travel (which we did by train). It was from near Hanover all the way north to the Danish border. The exact travel time I am unable to remember. I only know we spent many nights in tents, schools or if all were filled up, we spent the night outside in snow and mud.

The train was also packed with people, mostly refugees and farmers. We were wet and hungry most of the time. After a while the farmers unpacked their bundles and our eyes and mouths opened up. One lady asked us if we were hungry and all we could do was to let her hear our growling stomachs. She gave us her bread and even went around to other travelers to ask for some of their lunch. We finally arrived at our destination and were reunited with our father.

We did much better once we were a family again. We settled about 12 kilometers south of the Denmark border in a German farming community called Klixbull. We were still poor, so in order to eat, we raised chicken, rabbits, pigs, sheep and goats. We also had a very large garden, and raised all our vegetables. To buy staples, we took eggs to the store and traded these for flour, sugar salt, etc.

My oldest sister was married and had decided to stay with her husband and daughter in Vossen, near Berlin. Later, she fled East Germany in 1949 and stayed with us for a while. We had plenty of room, since we lived in a bunker; half in ground with the top half above. We six children went to school in Klixbull and to the High School in Niebull.

In 1957 I met my husband in Fulda. I had been trained as a seamstress and was working in Fulda at a Singer Sewing Machine store as a trainer; teaching new machine owners how to use the machine and

I also taught sewing in small towns around Fulda. My husband was an American soldier stationed in Fulda. He departed Germany in the spring of 1958 and I followed him a year later. It took that long to get all the paperwork and visas together and approved. I traveled to the U.S. on the SS Berlin. It took 10 days from Bremerhaven to New York. I arrived in the States (New York) around May 1, 1959 and about 10 days later we were married in Bedford, Pennsylvania. Since Harry stayed in the Army for 20 years, we traveled a lot. Harry was stationed in a number of different States and I was privileged to see a lot of the United States, which I dearly love and call home. In 1963 I was happy to become a United States Citizen.

We have two children, seven grandchildren, one great grandchild and one about to be born. The children of today have no idea how good they have it. As children, we had no TV and only the lucky had one radio for the entire family. At Christmas, we were lucky to get a family game; maybe our doll got a new dress, or the buggy received a new coat of paint.

All my brothers and sisters have also been married over 50 years except for the youngest sister. She will celebrate her Golden Wedding Anniversary in 2015.

Rose

I was born on February 24th in 1930, in Freising, a town in Bavaria in southern Germany. My family consisted of my father Mathias and mother Katharina, two brothers and myself. Before we were born, there was a little sister who died at the age of five of an undiagnosed illness. We were a farm family, and father, mother, and the children all worked in the fields as soon as we were able; from morning until night, since this was the way to support our family. Father's unmarried sister lived with us and did the housework, therefore freeing mother to work in the fields.

Father had a contract with a military hospital to provide them with different kinds of potatoes which were grown on our farm. The hospital took all the large potatoes and the small ones were ours to eat and also to feed to the pigs. There was no machinery in those days and it was intensive hand labor for all. I remember a family on the next smaller farm who had twelve children and they were always hungry.

The countryside was beautiful with the Alps in the background, only we never got to go there because there was always work for us to do. Our days started at 6 am, and then time out for school and then work again, whatever there was for us to do. The school I attended was for girls only, and our teachers were nuns who lived in the convent. We were expected to attend church every Sunday and when we arrived in school on Monday morning, they asked if we had been and we surely were reluctant to admit that we had not been. Class discipline was very strict, and many times I felt the pain of a bamboo stick across my hands.

In 1940, when I was ten, I joined the BDM, Bund Deutscher Mädchen, an association of young girls somewhat like the Girl Scouts. At our meetings once a week, we had craft times, singing, and went out into the woods collecting various things for our crafts. Other times we would go to the mountains, which were a real treat, since we did not get to go there on our own. Older girls went into what was called 'Arbeitsdienst', work service, literally translated. At 17, they went to the Air Force as telephone operators and various other services. Some girls were also trained as 'house helpers' and then went to assist large families with work in the home and with children.

Father and other farmers would sometimes meet at a Gasthaus in town and talk about cattle prices and other farm related things. But the talk always got around to the war and one thing they all knew, you could talk about anything, but negative talk about Hitler was forbidden because it carried a harsh penalty. Of course, times were hard and since all the young able bodied men were in the war there was not much help available. At the military hospital there were many wounded soldiers and when they were healed and just not quite ready to go back to the front, they would sometimes come and work awhile on the farm.

In April 1945, we once heard a lot of noise far off. But the only time Freising was bombed was on the day one of my uncles was escorting a high Nazi official to the train station when the bomb hit and both were killed, also 500 others were killed during that attack. At other times during the war, we would be working in the fields raking the grass together, when planes dropped aluminum strips down on us and we had to work hard to remove them from the grass. The animals that ate the grass could not digest those strips of foil and it would possibly make them sick. At other times, we believe, the planes dropped potato bugs on the fields and those also had to be picked off before they destroyed the crops. A strange kind of warfare, no doubt, but I now realize that these insects were naturally occurring. Bug warfare would have been incredibly ineffective. (Editor's note: None of the Allies dropped potato bugs. This would have been considered ineffective compared to bombs which were readily available. Later in the 1950s in the Southeastern United States, the U.S. Agricultural Department did fly over and drop sterile Screw Worm Flies over cattle. The flies mate only once, and by making the males sterile with radiation, these incredibly destructive pests were completely eradicated from the southeast U.S.)

There was shooting from the planes and we ran into the woods as soon as we heard the planes approaching. These planes managed to hit many people with their shooting and those people were then quickly gathered up in wagons and carried to the town, many were dead but some were only wounded and survived. The dead were then taken to the cemetery and people came by to indentify the ones they knew, which was a very sad time, because we all knew everyone in town and many were relatives. It was a time of great upheaval in our little community and at times I wondered if it would ever end and if we would survive.

Just before the war ended, a plane came by one day and destroyed the bridge over the Isar River. It was our only way to go from some of the fields and the next bridge was 30 kilometers away. So we had a long way home that day. Our family also had a shelter in a little hill where potatoes and other things were stored and it served as a safe hideout when the planes came over and, of course no one knew whether or not the bombs would be dropped.

Then came the Sunday in 1945 when there was a lot of shooting nearby and we went to our shelter. One man, on his way to the shelter, did not run fast enough and was killed before he got there. I had a date that day, but because of the shooting we did not meet. As it turned out, the Americans were closing in on the town and everyone hid. My friend with whom I had a date was at home in town with his parents and when he heard the shooting looked out the window and was promptly shot dead. This same fate came to many others also in these last days of the war. Finally the war was over, but the only change was that we saw lots of American soldiers around with trucks and jeeps. Food was still scarce; we still had ration cards but some things were not to be had for any amount one might want to pay.

My brothers had been drafted, one was 14 and the other 17, and one went to a mountain division and the other to the Wehrmacht (the Army). One brother was a prisoner of war, and while there he met another man who was from Eastern Europe, who also was scheduled for release at the same time. But since he had no address to go to, he was not going to be released. My brother offered him a home on our farm and the man gladly accepted, and they both came home, skinny and hungry. His name was Hans and later he married and had two boys. Later Hans was killed in a farm accident at age 37. During the war, the German military had hoarded food and all kinds of clothing, wine and other things in warehouses across the area. While the war was going on, those warehouses were heavily guarded and no one was allowed near. But as soon as the Americans came, all the people started for those warehouses and broke open the doors and took everything, rightfully so! Many people started making brandy, selling it to Americans. We had a still in the barn and one time a little pig got some of the brandy and was intoxicated a long time on homemade brandy. Eventually the Americans built a pontoon bridge across the Isar River where there was a big nearby park. Here they put up tents to house their troops.

We had an uncle whose two sons also went to war and both died, one fighting and the other starved to death in Russia. When the war was officially over, many German soldiers and civilians tried to go home and came through our town in ragged clothing and hungry, and sometimes a bicycle or two were missing; no doubt taken by someone who wanted to get home faster. Everyone was hungry and in need of clothes and the families with small children were especially pitiful. My mother was very kind and gave food to as many people as she was able. She tried to help wherever she could. It was a sad time.

My parents were older when they married, and as the custom is that when the owners of a farm get to an age where the work is harder and there are boys to inherit and of an age to be married, the parents retire and let the young men work the farm. This was the situation with my brother who was older than I and was the oldest son. He was already in his 30's and married. I was still a young girl who had to consider where I would spend my life. I went to a school where I learned housekeeping and cooking and general skills for homemaking.

At this time, the German Government let it be known that jobs were available with the Americans and I immediately applied and was hired to work for an American family. The pay was so much better than anywhere else and these were such nice people, different than any I had ever known before. They were very kind and generous with me and I enjoyed working there in their home. They had a little girl five years old and I still write to her and we met several years ago.

My grandmother had relatives in America who had left Germany in the early 1900's and settled in Kentucky. They came to visit and I became interested in America. My girlfriend and I saw in an American paper where they needed nannies and we applied and I was told of a position in New York with a family with two children and a baby; I would get $30 a week. That seemed like a lot of money to me and I decided to apply. After getting all my papers in order and a long boat ride, I arrived in New Jersey and traveled to the family. They had another woman who did the cleaning and the cooking and then I got the shock of my life, instead of $30 a week I was paid only $10.

On Labor Day, the family went to the ocean for vacation and I met a German girl who was from Rothenberg and worked for a family in New York. When she learned of what had happened to me with the money, she said "Why didn't I go to New York when the family she worked for returned from their vacation"? She knew another girl we where we could stay and we both started looking for another job. I found one working in a restaurant in Grand Central Station making $10 a day and I thought I had died and gone to heaven. That job I kept for many years. My girlfriend and I got a room for $10 a week, as I recall and I did not have to buy any food because working at the restaurant I could eat there and also take food home for the weekend. Every Friday I went to the bank and deposited my money and I thought I was rich! Life never had been so good before. One way I also saved money was that I walked the 40 blocks from where I lived to Grand Central Station to save a dime.

Before I left Germany, at the end of May in 1953, my close friend gave me a birthday party at the end of February. She had twin boys, and the American soldier who was the father had left, and she was by herself with those children. But some years later he came back and married her and they came to the States. At my birthday party she invited some other people, among them Grover, who was stationed in my hometown. We liked each other and dated for a few months until I had to leave in May. He told me about his home in Alabama and we talked about visiting. Our relationship continued by letters until the summer of 1954 when he came back to be stationed in Smyrna, Tennessee at the Air Force Base. When he went home to Alabama, I also came and we were married. It was really strange the way we started out and now we are married over 50 years. After we were married, I went back to New York and he went to the Air Base in Tennessee, until he was discharged in April 1955, and then came to New York. Before he came he went home to Alabama to buy a car and someone asked how he could pay for it since he did not have a job, he replied that his wife had a good job in New York, not to worry.

Where I worked in the restaurant, many of the workers from the railroad power station came to eat. I told them that my husband was coming and needed a job. Since Grover had worked at the power station in Germany while in the Air Force, he had experience, so when he applied, he had a job the next day. Life was indeed looking up for us. In 1957 our first boy was born. Grover took a job as a substitute teacher and kept the job at the railroad also. Then he went to school to get his teaching degree and finished with a masters degree and went on to be a teacher. All the while I continued to work at the restaurant for twenty years. We bought our first house in 1957. It was a five room house with a small apartment downstairs. We lived in the apartment and rented the other rooms out and made enough money to live payment free.

After I was not working anymore at the restaurant, our son mowed the neighbor's lawn. The homeowner, who was an attorney, asked me if I could help in their house with cleaning and cooking and taking his wife (who had cancer) to the doctor when she needed to go. They were already elderly, and after his wife died he was in ill health also. So he asked if I would continue to work for him and care for him and when he died he would leave me the house. He was as good as his word; that is exactly what happened. He died, after some years, and we inherited his house.

After that, I looked for another job and found one doing home care for an elderly lady whose son came once a week from the city to visit her. It was a 48 hour shift and then I came home and did what had to be done before I went to the other job caring for another lady for 48 hours. She died after 8 years. So life progressed until one day Grover said it was time to move to Alabama. We had visited there several times before and every time he was there he said he wanted to buy a farm.

The farm we did buy was not exactly what I had in mind because there were just too many hills and it was quite a long way to drive to town. I had envisioned flat land. We built our house and bought cattle and we worked on this farm until we just could not do it anymore. Our sons were grown, we had grandchildren, and here we were working from morning to night on a farm. After selling the house and most of the land, we moved to Athens and a house with only a ground floor and close to the stores and the church and all the other places we like to go. We have good neighbors and this is where we will stay. We have a good happy life.

Helga

My father was in the German Army during WW 1. My mother learned to be a dress maker, which in those days took four years of training. They were married in 1923 and lived with my mother's parents who had a large apartment in the city of Frankfurt am Main. I was born in 1924 and have vivid memories of my grandparents. My grandmother was a great story teller and entertained me often with her memories. After my dad got out of the army, he worked for an orthopedic institute, which later he became a co-owner. They made artificial legs and braces which were in demand after WW1. The business was in Eschersheim, a suburb of Frankfurt am Main. When the apartment above the business became available, we moved into it.

The apartment and business were in a very nice neighborhood containing big homes and lovely gardens. I still do not know exactly how the business came to be located there. At the time, I was five years old and went to four years of elementary school in Eschersheim. Later, I attended the Furtstenberger Middle School which was closer in to the city. During the winter, we went to school by streetcar, but in the spring and fall, we rode our bikes. I was an only child, but was never lonely since I had many good friends. Two of my friends were sisters and we spent all of our free time together; riding bikes, swimming and just playing schlagball (softball) together. From this period of my life, I remember only happy times.

Our teachers at the school were very strict. We stood up when they entered the room and only spoke when we were asked a question or had a comment directed to us by the teacher. There was not a friendly relationship between the teachers and the students. We studied French and English and had the same teacher for both subjects. For this class, we were not allowed to speak German. During this class, if we did not know a word, the teacher would explain it in the foreign language until we said that we understood it, again in the language that was being taught. I guess that he was ahead of his time, because today this method of language teaching is called "total immersion" instruction and is quite common today. I did not like the study of foreign languages because you have to study verbs, nouns and memorize vocabularies and at that time I would have preferred to be outside with my friends. Besides, I was much better in math and science.

After Hitler took over the government in 1933, he and his government controlled everything; the press, the teachers, etc. Everyone had to be careful what they said and to whom they said it. We were just young children and did not know any different than what the government said. I graduated from school in 1942 and at that time every young person was required by the Hitler government to give one year to the Fatherland before they could go to the university to further their education or even before they begin to study to learn a trade. Girls worked on a farm or with a family who had more than one child. I was lucky in this respect: in our neighborhood was a family with two children and the husband was away in the army. She was eligible for a helper and I went to their apartment in the morning but could go home each night. I only got a little spending money for my efforts, but it was nice. The thought was that girls would learn how to manage a household and take care of children. By this time in my life, we were experiencing many air raids. In the very beginning, we would just go to the basement of the building.

After that "Pflichtjahr" I was able to get a job at the "Postscheckamt". We operated big bookkeeping machines. I worked here during 1943 and 1944. During an air raid, the Postscheckamt was destroyed. During this raid, some of my coworkers and I had to run to a bunker about five blocks away. When we returned, we found that many of the other workers were killed in the basement of what was left of the building. Toward the end of the war, we spent much time in the bunkers because of the constant air raids. Our home had very little damage, but many times we were without water or electricity for extended periods. Since my mother was a skilled seamstress, she made all my clothes, sometimes out of other garments. At this time, you needed a ration coupon for everything; food, shoes, clothing etc. but somehow we managed.

Some of the first American troops to arrive occupied homes in our neighborhood. We were so very glad that the war was over for us, but there was still fighting in Berlin. I did hear Goebbels on the radio saying that this was just a temporary setback! He was still promoting total government lies.

In 1946 I started working for the US Army as a switchboard operator. This was four years after graduating from school and I had not spoken English in all those years, and had not wished to do so. In our case, we had learned British English in school which caused some misunderstandings with the GIs. With their different dialects, they were hard to understand, but I was young and eventually became used to them. My husband (to be) was in the Signal Corps and my boss. During the war, he had been stationed in North Africa. We were married in 1949 and were able to come back to the U.S. together.

It was very difficult in those days for a soldier to get permission to marry a German girl. I had to have an interview with his company commander and the chaplain. Additionally, I had to have a medical examination and he had to show proof that he could support me. After we were married, I was notified by the German Provisional

Government that I had lost my German citizenship, so until I received my American citizenship, I was technically a stateless person!

Upon our move to the U.S. my husband was stationed at Fort Bragg, NC. And then about eight months later he was sent to Korea. When he returned, we bought a house in Elizabethtown, PA. in 1951. Our only daughter was born in 1953.

We had 47 happy years together before my husband died in 1996.

CONCLUSION

If you have read this far, you have encountered truthful and disturbing accounts of the atrocities inflicted upon individuals and families as late as the mid 20th century, a time in our lives that we like to think of as a time of enlightenment. It was surely an exciting time with the advancements in technology, science and engineering and the early beginning of the electronic age. Yet the stories graphically detailed in this book are evidence of the unspeakable cruelty of some individuals and governments, and the corresponding nobility of the human spirit in others. It is also evidence that some individuals persevere and do survive in the presence of great adversity. Hildegard eloquently confirms that these stories represent not just isolated individuals, but are representative of entire classes of subjugated peoples during this era or human history. Their individual stories are thought provoking and an inspiration for us all.

We naturally ask ourselves; "Could our own government and society as a whole mimic the European experience?" We cannot be so sure how our society would respond. Each time this country experiences a local disaster of some magnitude, the press and TV are filled with images of crime and looting. I strongly suspect that we are not much different as a society from the mid 20th century societies whose behavior (as accounted in this book), we find so shocking. We like to think that we are a constitutional democracy with long established institutional safeguards. However, before the Nazi era, Germany was also a well established democracy.

If the question is asked; "Where have all the barbarians gone?", those great hordes in antiquity that sacked, looted, laid waste to the countryside, and put the sword to great cities such as Rome, etc. I strongly suspect that they are still interspersed among us, and are a sizeable portion of our society even at this the dawn of the 21st century.

Sometimes it seems that God in His infinite wisdom never shelters us from dysfunctional people or societies. It seems that no one is destined to spend this lifetime with only those with a true nobility of spirit. We have all encountered individuals that we can never count as friends and know of current day societies where we would not wish to live. Perhaps this is His plan to teach us the value of those spirits that exhibit true nobility and to show us the difference. However, we should not be consumed with despair by the vagrancies of human behavior; rather we should be vigilant to guard the freedoms that were secured for us by the sacrifice of much blood and treasure by true patriots over the centuries.

Mefford & Ehl

Livory for body,
Brandon Grotesque for subheads,
and Outage and Mr. Stalwart for headings and titling.
Written, compiled and proofed by M. Mefford & J. Ehl.
Cover and layout by J. Hall.
Printed in 2011.

CPSIA information can be obtained at www.ICGtesting.com
Printed in the USA
LVOW060406281211

261314LV00003B/2/P